Program Management Complexity

A Competency Model

ESI International Project Management Series

Series Editor

J. LeRoy Ward, Executive Vice President
ESI International
Arlington, Virginia

Program Management Complexity: A Competency Model
Ginger Levin, and J. LeRoy Ward
978-1-4398-5111-1

Project Management for Healthcare
David Shirley
978-1-4398-1953-1

Managing Web Projects
Edward B. Farkas
978-1-4398-0495-7

Project Management Recipes for Success
Guy L. De Furia
978-1-4200-7824-4

Building a Project Work Breakdown Structure: Visualizing Objectives, Deliverables, Activities, and Schedules
Dennis P. Miller
978-1-4200-6969-3

A Standard for Enterprise Project Management
Michael S. Zambruski
978-1-4200-7245-7

Determining Project Requirements
Hans Jonasson
978-1-4200-4502-4

The Complete Project Management Office Handbook, Second Edition
Gerard M. Hill
978-1-4200-4680-9

Practical Guide to Project Planning
Ricardo Viana Vargas
978-1-4200-4504-8

Other ESI International Titles Available from
Auerbach Publications, Taylor & Francis Group

PMP® Challenge! Fourth Edition
J. LeRoy Ward and Ginger Levin
ISBN: 978-1-8903-6740-4

PMP® Exam: Practice Test and Study Guide, Seventh Edition
J. LeRoy Ward
ISBN: 978-1-8903-6741-1

The Project Management Drill Book: A Self-Study Guide
Carl L. Pritchard
ISBN: 978-1-8903-6734-3

Project Management Terms: A Working Glossary, Second Edition
J. LeRoy Ward
ISBN: 978-1-8903-6725-1

Program Management Complexity

A Competency Model

Ginger Levin, PMP, PgMP

J. LeRoy Ward, PMP, PgMP

CRC Press
Taylor & Francis Group
Boca Raton London New York

CRC Press is an imprint of the
Taylor & Francis Group, an **informa** business

AN AUERBACH BOOK

To Morris Levin, for his continuing support and love

Ginger Levin, 2010

To Dick Rutledge and Ben Shaktman, whose advice forever changed my approach to presentations, leading to more fun and success than I ever thought possible

J. LeRoy Ward, 2010

Contents

Preface

As two of the first individuals to attain the Project Management Institute's (PMI) Program Management Professional (PgMP®) credential, we recognized in our studying of the PMI Program Management Standard (2006) and other key literature in the field, that little attention had been paid to the topic of complexity in program management. While both the first and second editions of the PMI's *The Standard for Program Management* (PMI, 2006, 2008b) note the importance of managing the projects in a program in a coordinated way to ensure that program benefits are achieved, neither edition addresses the complexity inherent in the interdependencies of such projects. Moreover, the topic of the complexity of programs has not been specifically addressed in the rather meager selection of books and other publications on program management now available in the marketplace. Additionally, there is little, if any, information available today identifying a set of competencies a program manager needs to possess to successfully complete his or her program and deliver the benefits desired by stakeholders. This book fills this void.

We offer a competency model based on more than 70 years of collective experience in the field, as well as drawing from other authoritative sources, that can help existing program managers assess where they can enhance their own skills, while also providing prospective program managers information so they, and others, can determine if they are ready to assume a program manager position. Finally, our model can be used by corporate and governmental organizations, universities, executives, and human resources professionals to determine program management training needs and other developmental approaches to ensure their staff members can successfully fulfill the role of program manager. After all, programs, with their focus on major and substantive organizational change, are becoming an increasingly more important component in organizations' portfolios. Someone has to "run" them, and that someone must have the requisite skills and competencies to do nothing short of an outstanding job.

We believe complexity is a phenomenon that has plagued and challenged many project and program managers in every industry sector and across all geographies. However, while much research has been devoted to complexity in terms of *project* management, limited research is available on complexity in *program* management not withstanding the fact that complexity is a recognized characteristic of program management. Perhaps this is because program management remains in its infancy as a profession as compared to project management. But programs are major assets to organizations driving organizational change throughout major business units. If such initiatives are seen mainly as a collection of projects, then resource allocation will be subpar, planning will be episodic, and there will be no one who understands the coherent "whole." As such, the organization stands a greater chance of being unsuccessful, paying more money, and taking more time, than if the projects were managed in a coordinated way.

Additionally, and even when managed in a coordinated way, as the level of complexity increases in a program, the ability of the program manager and his or her team to deliver stated benefits can be, and often is, negatively impacted. Far too often, people do not understand the level of complexity they face until they are "right in the middle of it." Manifestations of negative impact include deteriorating team morale, sponsor and client dissatisfaction, cost and time overruns, and poor requirements management, to name several. Such negative impact has been quantified by many organizations and reveals that hundreds of millions of dollars are being misspent as a result of poor program management practices.

This book, and the development of its accompanying competency model for program managers, was prepared to emphasize the following areas:

- How can a program manager identify the nature and components of complexity in his or her program such that it can be managed successfully and the program will deliver its intended benefits?
- What are the key competencies required of the program manager for success?

In other words, if a program manager can recognize the elements of complexity early on during the defining and initiating stages of a program, can he or she apply certain and specific competencies and management techniques to ensure that such complexity is not a detriment to the program? Moreover, once recognized, what steps can a program manager take to use such complexity to his or her best advantage? And, how can a competency model assist program managers in successful delivery of program benefits and products, services, or results?

The book is organized first with a literature review of program and project management complexity. It then presents an overview of a competency model for program managers, divided into performance competencies and personal competencies. The performance competencies are organized according to the six domains of program management, while the eight personal competencies are based on research plus a limited survey by Program Management Professionals (PgMPs®), who also assisted in its validation.

Following the model are three assessment instruments that include questions to assess one's own competency as a program manager, questions one can use if considering program management as a career, as well as questions an organization can use to determine the knowledge, skills, and competencies of the program managers in the organization to then chart a path for professional growth and continuous improvement. These questions also are contained on the accompanying CD-ROM to this book.

Guidance on methods to implement the model for use by individuals who are program managers, are aspiring to be program managers, or by the organization for its program professionals is provided.

Program management is an exciting field but there is a lot at stake: time, money, your organization's reputation, and *your* personal reputation. This work is our attempt to provide some guidance and assistance in helping to ensure that we are all successful with our programs. Let us know what you think.

Ginger Levin, DPA, PMP, PgMP
Lighthouse Point, Florida

J. LeRoy Ward, PMP, PgMP
New York, New York

About the Authors

Dr. Ginger Levin is a senior consultant and educator in project management. Her specialty areas are portfolio management, program management, the Project Management Office, knowledge management, metrics, and maturity assessments. She is certified as a PMP®, PgMP®, and as an *OPM3* Assessor and Consultant. She was the second person in the world to receive the PgMP.

In addition, Dr. Levin is an adjunct professor for the University of Wisconsin-Platteville, where she teaches in its M.S. in Project Management Program and for SKEMA (Esc Lille) University, France, in its project management program at the masters and doctoral level. Also, she is a Visiting Professor for RMIT in Melbourne, Australia.

In consulting, she has served as project manager in numerous efforts for Fortune 500 and public-sector clients, including UPS, Citibank, the U.S. Food and Drug Administration, General Electric, SAP, EADS, John Deere, Schreiber Foods, TRW, the New York City Transit Authority, the U.S. Joint Forces Command, and the U.S. Department of Agriculture.

Prior to her work in consulting, she held positions of increasing responsibility with the U.S. government, including the Federal Aviation Administration, Office of Personnel Management, and the General Accounting Office.

She is the co-author of *Implementing Program Management: Forms and Templates Aligned with the Standard for Program Management,* Second Edition (2008); *Project Portfolio Management: Tools & Techniques; Metrics for Project Management; Achieving Project Management Success Using Virtual Teams; The Advanced Project Management Office: A Comprehensive Look at Function and Implementation; People Skills for Project Managers; Essential People Skills for Project Managers; The Business Development Capability Maturity Model;* and *ESI's PMP Challenge! PMP Study Guide* and the *PgMP Study Guide* (along with J. LeRoy Ward). Her book entitled *Interpersonal Skills for Portfolio, Program, and Project Managers* also was published in 2010.

Dr. Levin received her doctorate in Information Systems Technology and Public Administration from The George Washington University, and received the Outstanding Dissertation Award for her research on large organizations. She also was inducted into Phi Alpha Alpha, the National Honorary Society for Public Affairs and Administration.

J. LeRoy Ward, Executive Vice President, is responsible for ESI's worldwide product offerings and international partnerships. Complementing a 17-year career with four U.S. federal agencies, Ward has delivered project management programs to clients around the world.

A noted author and speaker, Ward has served on the adjunct faculties of The George Washington University and American University, presenting courses in remote sensing, cartography, computer systems management, and information systems. He has authored numerous articles and publications, including the *Dictionary of Project Management Terms (3rd ed.);* the *PMP® Exam Practice Test and Study Guide, PMP® Challenge!,* and the *PgMP® Exam Practice Test and Study Guide* (with Ginger Levin); a set of audio CDs entitled *Conversations on Passing the PMP® Exam* (with Carl Pritchard); and *ProjectFRAMEWORK, a Project Management Maturity Model* (with multiple authors, including Ginger Levin). His articles have appeared in *PMNetwork, Chief Learning Officer,* and *Project Manager Today (U.K.).* A popular and dynamic presenter, he speaks frequently on project management and related topics at professional association meetings and conferences around the world.

Ward holds B.S. and M.S. degrees from Southern Connecticut State University in geography and an MSTM degree, with distinction, in Computer Systems Management from American University, where he was inducted into Phi Alpha Alpha, the National Honorary Society for Public Affairs and Administration. He is an alumnus of the General Services Administration's Trail Boss Program (for major systems acquisitions) and the Federal Executive Institute.

Ward is a member of several technical societies, including the American Geographical Society, the American Society of Training and Development, the International Project Management Association, and the Project Management Institute where he is certified as a Project Management Professional (PMP—Number 431) and a Program Management Professional (PgMP), one of the first to earn the credential.

Overview

Complexity is a phenomenon that has plagued, confounded, and challenged many program managers across all industry sectors and geographies. In short, as the level of complexity increases in a program (defined as a business initiative comprising a group of related projects that are best managed in a coordinated way to achieve stated business benefits), the ability of the program manager and his or her team to deliver stated benefits can be, and often is, negatively impacted. Manifestations of negative impact include deteriorating team morale, sponsor and client dissatisfaction, cost and time overruns, and poor requirements management, to name several. Such negative impact has been quantified, in particular in the information technology industry, by firms and organizations such as Standish (2007). These reports reveal that hundreds of millions of dollars are being misspent as a result of poor program management practices.

Our goal is to help bring these poor practices to an end. Accordingly, this book focuses on answering the following questions:

- How can a program manager identify the nature and components of complexity in his or her program such that it can be managed successfully, and the program will deliver its intended benefits?

- What are the key competencies required of the program manager for success?
- How can a competency model assist program managers, aspiring program managers, and organizations?

Our thesis is simple: If a program manager can recognize the elements of complexity early on during the defining and initiating stages, he or she will be able to apply certain and specific competencies and management techniques to ensure that such complexity is not a detriment to the program. Moreover, once recognized, there are certain steps a program manager can, and should, take to use such complexity to his or her best advantage. And, finally, a competency model can be used as a guide to recruit, train, and develop a program manager such that he or she is successful in delivering stated program benefits, products, services, and results.

1

COMPLEXITY IN PROGRAM MANAGEMENT

Background

Complexity, as a discrete topic, has been studied and analyzed for years by many writers and thinkers. There are numerous books and articles on the subject, and, broadly speaking, it appears there is beginning to be some degree of consensus as to what complexity is and how it is defined. Moreover, the literature in project management is quite rich with many books, articles, dissertations, refereed papers, and theses being written on all aspects of the discipline, including identifying and managing project complexity.

Project management has emerged in the past ten to 15 years as a legitimate discipline with its own body of knowledge, standards, and methodologies. As we go to press, there are more than 300 colleges and universities around the world offering courses or degrees in the subject. Additionally, according to the Project Management Institute (PMI 2010), the largest association of project managers in the world, to date there are approximately 400,000 people who are certified as a Project Management Professional (PMP®).

The same cannot be said for the field of program management, defined by the PMI (2008d) as "a group of related projects managed in a coordinated way to obtain benefits and control not available from managing them individually. Programs may include elements of related work outside the scope of the discrete projects in the program" (p. 5). To date, there are only about 500 people certified by the PMI (2010) as a Program Management Professional (PgMP®). Very few, if any, universities offer courses in the area, and there are no generally accepted bodies of knowledge or methodologies in the field, save for what a specific corporation or organization might have developed for internal use. The one standard on the subject was published by the PMI, while the Office of Government Commerce (2007), a part of the U.K. government, has published a "guide" entitled *Managing Successful Programmes*, which has an associated credential entitled the MSP. In short, program management has a long way to go to catch up to its "cousin," project management. And additional attention is required for the reasons discussed below.

Programs are more varied in nature than projects and can be materially different along many dimensions. For example, it is widely held as conventional fact that a project has a beginning and an end. Yet, many programs have no stated end, let alone an end date.

> For example, an annual construction program, such as one in which one of the authors worked on for the U.S. Bureau of Indian Affairs (BIA), will never end so long as the BIA elects to educate Indian children located on the more than 400 reservations in the United States.

A second and material difference is that a program, by definition, can have elements of operational activities associated with it (e.g., maintenance and operations of Indian schools). By definition, a project does not include such activities. Complexity in program management then may arise from the interrelationships and interconnections between and among its constituent projects and non-project work, in addition to the varied sources that have been described in the literature as causing complexity within the individual projects themselves. As well, programs must contend with competition in the marketplace; in technology; in the products, services, and results of the program; and in the performing organization as well as the client organization. These interconnections and interrelationships are explored in this book.

Working with private-sector companies in all industry verticals and geographies, and also with government agencies and nonprofit organizations around the world, we note that there is no commonly held definition of what a program is; accordingly, the definition of program management tends to be "murky" as well. In short, it seems to be unique to whatever organization is practicing the discipline. Additionally, our literature review did not discover any level of substantive treatment related to the issue of complexity in programs and, as an extension, on how to manage such complexity. There are, however, an increasing number of articles and books that address project complexity, but projects as stand-alone entities.

We have concluded, therefore, that the area of complexity as it relates specifically to programs is in need of further study. Accordingly, this book is intended to add to what little body of knowledge exists and should help program managers identify complexity and ways to deal with it using a competency model as an aid.

Definition of Complexity and Its Key Concepts

It is important to note that even the word "complexity" is difficult to understand. Geraldi (2008) states that "mastering complexity is not a new challenge but an old challenge that is being increasingly recognized and accepted" (p. 4). She points out that while projects and project management are associated with complexity, many have difficulty understanding the concept and, as such, do not look upon a project as a complex system, with very negative consequences. Projects are complex because they represent something unique. And because they are unique, they have an element of uncertainty with regard to their execution that often results in re-work and added time and costs. Often there is insufficient time to make decisions, and it is easy to become involved in the details, losing sight of the overall goals and objectives. This need for timely decision making may lead to mistakes, especially if the goals are not explicit, the team has not worked together before (or is in the forming stage), and there is a large number of stakeholders struggling to comprehend a significant amount of information.

Other key concepts that lead to complexity include politics, new technology, the size of the project, involvement of other organizational units, a large quantity of information sources, a low maturity level in project management, and new processes to consider. The list is long in the project environment, and many of these concepts tend to be overlooked. Partly this is because complexity is not well defined or noted in the field. Cicmil, Cooke-Davies, Crawford, and Richardson (2009) point out this dilemma as they note that "dictionary definitions are not particularly helpful" after stating that discussion of "complex projects is bound to encounter risks inherent in the use of language" (p. 19).

Work on complexity originated during the mid-1980s at New Mexico's Santa Fe Institute. Distinguished professionals in the fields of particle physics, microbiology, archaeology, astrophysics, paleontology, zoology, botany, and economics came together with similar questions to study and debate the concept of complexity in the life, physical, and social sciences. Their groundbreaking work, as well as substantive research that followed, has offered a definition of complexity theory as the study of how order, structural patterns, and novelty arise from extremely complicated, apparently chaotic systems, and conversely, how complex behavior and structure emerge from simple underlying rules (Cooke-Davies, Cicmil, Crawford, and Richardson 2007). This definition was also used in the Cicmil et al. (2009) study. The name largely attributed to the advent of this new science of complexity is Prigogine, a 1977 Nobel Laureate in Chemistry, whose landmark book, *Order Out of Chaos,* explored the nature of change through "dissipative structures," otherwise known as open systems (Jaafari 2003, p. 48). Thomas and Mengel (2008) note, however, that the translation from the scientific area to management theory has been slow at best.

Relevant and key concepts associated with complexity theory include the following.

Nonlinearity

Nonlinearity is a state in which there is an interaction between two or more elements in a system that could not have been predicted at the time the system was designed (Ivory and Alderman 2005). This concept is best expressed by the title of a paper authored by Edward Lorenz, a meteorologist at the Massachusetts Institute of Technology and presented at the 1979 Annual Meeting of the American Association for the Advancement of Science: "Predictability: Does the Flap of a Butterfly's Wings in Brazil Set Off a Tornado in Texas?" Using advanced and powerful computer models of weather systems, Lorenz discovered one important aspect of how nonlinearity affects the weather, which he termed the principle of "sensitive dependence on initial conditions." In other words, he discovered how minute changes, or small perturbations, can have major and unpredictable consequences in nonlinear systems. This phenomenon is called the "Butterfly" effect after the title of his paper (Cooke-Davies et al. 2007).

Self-Organization and Emergence

It has been noted that a physical, biological, or social system (such as the one in which projects and programs are managed) has a distinct tendency, when left undisturbed, to organize in ways that are often unpredictable. Such spontaneous behavior often gives rise to new patterns of behavior. The emergent properties of these systems allow for novelty and innovation, and provide a credible account of how diversity and variety arise in order to allow evolution to happen (Cooke-Davies et al. 2007). This concept has profound implications in the management of complex projects and programs, especially when the core team members, as well as extended team members, are not colocated and function in a virtual environment.

Complex Adaptive Systems (CAS)

This concept is central to understanding complexity and ways to deal with it. A CAS arises from a self-organizing system, noting that such a system has the capacity to learn from experience. It is this ability to adapt to its surroundings that ensures its survival in the face of a changing environment. In order for an entity to qualify as a CAS, it must meet four tests:

1. It is comprised of many agents or building blocks acting in parallel; it is not hierarchically controlled.
2. The building blocks continually shuffle, generating multiple levels of organization and structure.
3. It is subject to the second law of thermodynamics, exhibiting entropy and winding down over time unless replenished with energy.
4. It exhibits a capacity for pattern recognition and employs said capacity to anticipate the future and learn to recognize seasonal change (Pascale 1999).

Additionally, it consists of a number of independent agents guided by their own rules of behavior and a scheme shared with other groups; complex adaptive systems are thus spontaneous and self-reorganizing (Thomas and Mengel 2008).

Defining Project Complexity and Its Key Factors

In 1996, the North Atlantic Treaty Organization (NATO) sponsored an Advanced Research Workshop focusing on the topic of *Managing and Modeling Complex Projects*. The workshop was based on the following premises: Projects are becoming complex, traditional project management methods are proving inadequate, and new methods of analysis and management are needed (Williams 1999).

The first step in attempting to develop tools and techniques to manage complex projects is to define what a complex project is. Baccarini (1996), citing work done in the construction industry, proposes that project complexity be defined as something with varied but interrelated parts within it and can be operationalized in terms of differentiation and interdependency. He asserts that this definition can be applied to any project dimension relevant to the project management process, including organization, technology, environment, information, decision making, and systems. In this context, then, complexity is a distinctly different concept from other project characteristics such as size and uncertainty. Baccarini also suggests that the two types of project complexity most commonly referred to in project management texts are organizational and technological complexity.

Both organizational and technological complexity manifest themselves in the forms of differentiation and interdependency. Differentiation in organizational complexity has two dimensions: vertical (depth of organizational hierarchy) and horizontal (number of organizational units and task structure). Differentiation as it relates to technological complexity includes such characteristics as number and diversity of inputs, number of specialties, and number of separate tasks to produce the project's end product. Interdependency can encompass the linkage or interconnections between tasks, within a network of tasks, between teams, or between different technologies. Managing such organizational and technological complexity requires integration defined as coordination, communication, and control.

Williams (1999), citing prior research by other noted experts, expands Baccarini's definition of project complexity by including the concept of uncertainty, stating that projects can be classified by two parameters: how well defined the goals are and how well defined the methods are of achieving those goals. Uncertainty in either of these areas will add to project complexity because the fundamental building blocks of project management will not be known. Ambiguity has also been cited as a factor in creating complexity in projects (Helm and Remington 2005).

Two other factors also add to project complexity: the complexity of the product to be produced by the project, as well as the fact that projects have tended to become more time constrained over the years. Product complexity can be equated to technological complexity; time constraints are altogether different. As organizations rush to be the first to bring their products to market, the overall project timeline shrinks, causing project managers to execute more tasks in parallel, in an overlapping manner, or concurrently, to the greatest extent practicable. This requires a completely different management approach, and as such "fast-tracking" the schedule brings with it certain inherent risks not found when such a method is not employed. The field of concurrent engineering, for example, has emerged as a result of the need to reduce cycle time to be first to market (Williams 1999).

Some note that project complexity is in the "eye of the beholder" (Bannan 2006, p. 78). This concept explains that project managers have strategies they can use to handle complex projects and states that a complex project is one that is large and has dependencies, a deadline, and a tight budget. A key strategy for project managers then to use is a stakeholder analysis to ensure there are no political ramifications and to identify a smaller group to engage when decisions must be made. This approach, in effect, uses concepts of that of a Work Breakdown Structure (WBS) in which each decision is decomposed until the "right" people are selected to assist in identifying the key information required to make and execute the decision. It requires project managers to have a thorough understanding of the various project deliverables because a project that is considered complex will usually have many milestones to meet. As noted by Cable in Bannan (2006), this approach requires the project manager to have competencies in leadership and motivation.

Maylor, Vidgen, and Carver (2008) suggest that complexity has a bipartite nature as it has both structural (i.e., stable qualities) as well as dynamic qualities. For example, a structural dimension would be phrased as "Are the requirements clear?", whereas its dynamic equivalent would be phrased as "How frequently do the requirements change?"

Project complexity has also been defined as the degree of clarity of goals and goal paths, and the propensity for goals and goal paths to change during the project life cycle (Helm and Remington 2005).

Modeling and Managing Project Complexity

Based on research conducted in several workshops with practicing project managers, an initial model of managerial complexity for projects (MODeST) has been offered (Maylor, Vidgen, and Carver 2008). The MODeST model suggests that there are five dimensions or characteristics of project complexity that a project manager must be concerned about: mission, organization, delivery, stakeholders, and team. Each of these five dimensions is further subdivided into specific areas for a project manager to consider when managing a complex project.

We did not find any other "models" of complexity; however, the literature does include many ideas as to where project managers should focus their efforts when confronted with a complex project. For example, in research conducted on complex construction projects, integration needs to be a key area of focus (Baccarini 1996); project managers need to concentrate on managing wider organizational teams, complex supply chains, and relationships with other stakeholders (Alderman, Ivory, and Vaughan 2005); a strong and influential project sponsor is important in such endeavors, most particularly on large infrastructure projects (Helm and Remington 2005); understanding the reactions of various groups of people to rapid technological, social, economic, and global change is central to understanding how to manage complexity (Jaafari 2003); governance regimes, especially for infrastructure megaprojects, need to be able to deal with emergent complexity, changing as the project development project unfolds, including submitting the projects for scrutiny (Miller and Hobbs 2005); and the multinodal characteristics of projects, where there are multiple centers of influence, should cause project managers to adopt less of a strong top-down project management system and instead focus on bottom-up approaches as well (Ivory and Alderman 2005).

Also, a recent addition is the College of Complex Project Managers (CCPM), which has its own standard, stating in its competency standard that "it describes people, especially the foundation for project managers, to deal with complex projects effectively in order to add increasing value to not only the work involved but also to the world" (Dombkins 2006). Although there is debate about the purpose of this College (Whittey and Maylor 2009), it does show increasing recognition of complexity within project management.

Furthermore, Cicmil et al. (2009) conclude that there are three key aspects relevant to project complexity. First, there is the ambiguity that often exists in projects concerning performance criteria and differing understandings of what constitutes project success. Second, there is the unpredictability of the future and how project work is continually unfolding, which leads to anxiety because planning done early in the project becomes the basis for later execution, monitoring, and control. And, third, there are the different social interactions, interfaces, and relationships that exist on projects, especially those in which team member backgrounds, value systems, and positions of power differ. They conclude that these three aspects are interrelated and are a consequence of the processes involving human relationships in a project environment. Gareis and Nankivel (2007) note that "project management is all about managing complexities. The more experience you have, the more competencies you will have acquired along the way. And, you'll gain the potential to take over not only larger projects but also programs, and not only manage a single project but the strategic leadership of a company's entire portfolio" (p. 7).

Program Complexity

The literature clearly shows that managerial complexity is a far more extensive construct than previously described in the field. Programs obviously are not projects, and there are fundamental differences between the two.

Current program and project management bodies of knowledge or methodologies are incomplete and do not address complexity in any meaningful or practical way. In fact, there is a highly Tayloristic one-best-way approach that most methodologies employ, which is inconsistent with the contextual diversity that managers face (Maylor, Vidgen, and Carver 2008). In fact, project failures continue to occur in the face of an ever-increasing number of bodies of knowledge. As such, traditional tools such as the Program Evaluation Review

Technique (PERT) fail at the most fundamental level to address the dynamics of complex adaptive systems such as that which is evident in complex projects. Recognizing the limitations of such tools in addressing complexity and associated challenges, software developers for certain projects are using the Agile method. Characterized by time-boxed phases in which components of systems are developed and tested prior to moving to the next phase, Agile offers an alternative to the traditional approach to managing a project employing the well-known "waterfall" project management life cycle.

The literature thus seems to fall short in two aspects. The first is that much of the research conducted on complexity focuses on large infrastructure, construction, or traditional architect and engineering projects. While we do not dispute the complexity inherent in these projects, certainly projects such as global drug development, large-scale telecommunications design and implementation, software development, and systems integration deserve treatment and would probably offer additional perspectives on the nature of complexity and ways to deal with it.

Second, and very central to this book, is that the literature addressing the concept of *program* complexity (as compared to *project* complexity) is only available in the most indirect and tangential manner. For example, if one were to closely examine the MODeST model of project complexity, there are certain questions enumerated that the model's authors suggest a project manager consider when managing a complex project that one could assume might be applied to programs. These include

- Are there competing priorities between projects?
- Are there interdependencies between projects?
- Is delivery to a non-project-based organization?
- Does the project involve organizational change? (Maylor et al. 2008)

However, there are no other questions that one could reasonably infer to apply to the program complexity, and it is not altogether clear that the authors had programs in mind when they phrased the above.

Programs are different from projects for the simple reason that it takes multiple, related projects, and possibly non-project work, to comprise a program. This very basic difference presents us with an opportunity to explore the nature of complexity as it pertains to this unique management structure. In so doing, we have identified the key competencies required of the program manager, following that of a project manager but expanded to programs, as described in the PMI (2007) competency framework for project managers.

Program management, while well established in countries such as the United States, the United Kingdom, and in the Australian government typically in the area of defense program management, has only recently been of interest to the commercial arena. In the United Kingdom, for example, Partington, Pellegrinelli, and Young (2005) state that while project management is well recognized, at the same time, corporate program management is emerging. They describe corporate program management as "structures and processes that are used to co-ordinate and direct the multiple inter-related projects that together constitute an organization's strategy" (p. 87). Their research focuses on what is necessary for one to be successful in program management and how the role differs from that of the project manager, emphasizing that simply because someone was a competent project manager does not mean he or she will be good at program management. Their conclusions show that program management is different for many reasons, and it requires a blend of interpersonal skills, personal credibility, and political awareness, among other things, to be competent in this area. In their research, they posed three questions, which we believe are answered by this competency model.

Pellegrinelli et al. (2007) note that "the widespread use of programme management has outpaced our ability to grasp and codify

Partington, Pellegrinelli, and Young (2005) state that leaders responsible for providing a succession system of program managers must answer three key questions:

1. What are the qualities that distinguish an effective program manager?
2. How can one assess whether the manager possesses these competencies?
3. Can competence of program managers be developed, or is the solution to rely on processes to select or de-select these managers?

a complex and subtle phenomenon" (p. 41). They explain that program management is used as the way to focus on planned change as it is the way to move forward especially in complex change initiatives. However, they also state that people working in program management spend time wondering what others in the field mean by this work.

However, we note that within the past several years, many large organizations have expressed a need to develop methodologies and approaches to deal with programs and program management, including developing competency models for program managers. Thus, the time appears ripe to conduct research into this emerging field. The model we present in this book is a beginning to describe the importance of competency in program management, which builds on the work done by Cicmil et al. (2009). That research had an inherent focus on project management and, by extension, program management, including delving into the area of social science.

2

A COMPETENCY MODEL FOR PROGRAM MANAGERS

Introduction

Programs can vary from an internal initiative to improve overall program management processes, or to increase maturity in project, program, and portfolio management, to the implementation of an enterprise resource planning (ERP) program or the building of a new aircraft or submarine. The need for competent program managers who can initiate, plan, execute, monitor, and control these complex undertakings has never been greater. An increasing number of the authors' clients expect to initiate improvement in their program management capabilities, including training, professional development activities, methodologies, and processes, in the next two years. In fact, there has never been a better time to be a program manager.

Table 2.1 shows the differences between project management and program management at a high level (Ward 2009). The differences noted are not an "either/or" binary reference; in fact, the differences should be read as two ends of a continuum.

Crawford (2005) notes that different levels of people perceive competency in different ways. She explains that senior managers often resist involvement by project managers in practices concerning strategy, definition, integration, and communication. Senior managers consider these practices as over-arching while the focus of the project manager is (or perhaps should be) on time, cost, scope, and procurement, thus confirming the difference noted in Table 2.1 on a more singular, narrow focus at the project manager level. The nature of the specific project is another concern, as reported by Einsiedel in her study (reported in Crawford 2005), in which project management effectiveness "depends on a wide variety of factors, some of which

Table 2.1   Differences between Program Management and Project Management

AREA	PROJECT MANAGEMENT	PROGRAM MANAGEMENT
Focus	Nonstrategic	Strategic
Objectives	Singular	Multiple
Extent of Change	Narrow	Broad
Benefits Realization	Once	Incremental
Deliverable Complexity	Low	High
Deliverable Quantity	Few	Many
Overall Time Scale	Rigid	Loose
Scope Change	Exceptional	Desirable
Functional Diversity	Minimal	Multidisciplinary

have little or nothing to do with the managers' personal ability or motivation" (p. 11).

The U.S. Government Accountability Office (GAO 2005) conducted a survey based on the U.S. Department of Defense's (DoD) long-established program management function to determine whether the DoD's program management performance was mature enough to be able to deliver the intended benefits from the funds allocated to it. The GAO study compared program management practices from large corporations to those of the DoD. It noted there were nine environmental factors that the companies in the survey found were essential to program management success:

1. Use investment strategies
2. Use evolutionary development
3. Match requirements to resources
4. Match the right people to the program
5. Use knowledge-driven development decisions
6. Empower program managers
7. Demand accountability
8. Require tenure
9. Continue senior leadership support

It is interesting to note the emphasis in this study on matching the right people to the program. This observation, among other factors, led to our development of this competency model for program managers.

Partington et al. (2005) explain that an interpretive approach is required, which we have tried to create. They describe traditional approaches to competence as work oriented and worker oriented. Work oriented goes back to that of Taylor and focuses on the work involved, rather than the actual person who is responsible for the work. In fact, this description is the focus of the PMI (2008a) and also the U.K.'s Association for Project Management (2006), in which lists of relevant topics, activities, performance indicators, and knowledge are used to help guide project management work. This approach, however, does not focus on the attributes needed of the person responsible for doing the work.

The worker-related studies, on the other hand, address this gap by focusing on the person involved to generalize the knowledge, skills, and attributes that one requires. Partington et al. (2005) caution that such an approach may result in findings that are too generic and abstract, and therefore not relevant to specific organizations. Accordingly, they present an alternative interpretive approach focusing on what the manager conceives of the work and how the workers conceive it. They studied five large U.K. firms from different sectors and conducted interviews with those responsible for program management. They also shadowed these individuals to see the actual work they did over a two-day period. Other interviews were conducted with the program manager's sponsors, clients, and peers. Their model concluded that program management was a concept that was "difficult to pin down" (p. 94). This conclusion was based on differences between programs in the different sectors of the study.

Thomas and Mengel (2008) make the link between complexity in project management and competency. They assert that as organizations become more complex, it is necessary to have an understanding as to what is meant by complexity and point out the numerous interrelationships to consider, such as the environments (both internal and external), the cultural considerations, the competition, and the customers, all of which make it necessary for practitioners to make decisions based on many variables that are not known. Their research emphasizes that project managers may not be able to handle complex projects and discusses the need for "master project managers" to have competencies in areas including shared leadership, social competence and emotional intelligence, communications, organizational political skills, and vision, values, and beliefs. As a result, more emphasis is needed in these interpersonal skills rather than a strict focus on the tools and techniques in the *PMBOK® Guide* (or other project management guides and standards) to be able to respond to the environmental complexity and change in many projects. Their research also emphasizes the fact that the need for personal competencies is even more applicable to the program setting as each program is complex from the moment it is initiated, all the way through to its closing given that uncertainty and change are prevalent.

Patanakul and Milosevic (2009) discuss several competencies needed to lead a group of multiple projects, including but not limited to having an innovative thinking style, minimizing the time required to switch to another project, simultaneously leading multiple teams, and knowing the most appropriate conflict management techniques. In their study, they focus on management of a number of multiple projects in which projects are grouped for greater management efficiency, but yet lead to stronger interdependencies as they are managed by the same person. They define program management as "the centralized, coordinated management of a group of goal-related projects to achieve the program's strategic objectives and benefits" (p. 218).

Using a case study approach with six different organizations, the competencies they describe include managing, communicating, problem solving, multitasking and maintaining focus, identifying and managing risks, and adapting one's style to accommodate the variety of people who are working on different teams. They further note the importance of the manager's tenure with the organization and the ability to have a solid foundation in project management as well as business competencies such as understanding clients, being able to integrate multiple activities and departments, and having a sense of the overall business. Additionally, they describe internal traits, such as being organized, disciplined, proactive, mature, and self-controlled, all of which contribute to being able to interface with a diverse group of stakeholders in a short period of time. As such, they conclude that both hard and soft competencies are required.

Gregory Balestrero, president and chief executive officer of the Project Management Institute (2010), states, "In 2008, PMI commissioned a study by the *Economist* Information Unit that interviewed almost 600 senior executives of national, multinational and global companies. Most of them said they did not think their organization's talent management was good enough." In this study, he explained the following:

- 95% said, "Skilled talent is needed for success"
- 75% said, "My organization lacks execution skills critical to success"
- 55% said, "Our senior executives leave talent selection to unit managers"
- 43% said, "Our performance evaluation is based on financial indicators only" (not on ensuring tomorrow's talent)

Balestrero further states:

Asked what they needed most from new **employees**, they said: the ability to execute projects successfully. (Who do we know who specializes in that skill?)

Asked what capability they most wanted **their companies** to have, they said: the ability to *carry out* the changes we know we need to make. (Who do we know who specializes in carrying out change?)

The most important organizational capability was to implement strategic change. Moving forward, Balestrero notes the increase in program management over project management and the requirement for increased insight into how programs emerge and develop, as well as the need to be able to manage a common pool of resources across programs in organizations.

Model Development

To begin the development of this model, an informal survey was conducted of members in an online PgMP® group as to the competencies they felt were required of program managers. Following the theme of that by Cicmil et al. (2009), the majority addressed the need to recognize the complex processes of interaction. Suggestions included

- Stakeholder management
- Communications planning

- Effective listening
- Social responsibility
- Effective written and oral communications at all levels
- Long-range strategic planning
- Relationship building and management—both vertical and horizontal
- Mapping business strategy to program objectives
- Interpersonal skills
- Negotiation skills
- Strategic thinking to set the vision
- Tactical planning to sell the vision
- Financial acumen
- Benefits management
- Strategic integration management
- Leadership

It is interesting to note that those polled did not include "technical" competency as being needed. Perhaps it is implied, and the ones above are those "in addition" to the technical competence of the program manager. However, in presentations given by the authors over many years, when a similar question is asked of the audience, the response is very much the same as above. When collectively asked about technical competence, there is always a range of opinions. Some opine that a certain amount of technical competence in the nature of the program is helpful, but not altogether required in many circumstances. Yet others vehemently argue that the program manager be a technical expert in the work of the program.

Using this small sample, the conclusions of the GAO report, the need for hard and soft competencies from Patanakul and Milosevic, plus our own experience as program managers and PgMPs, we developed the Levin-Ward competency model, shown below, following the PMI (2007) competency framework for project management. We also wanted to make it generic enough that it could be used, in whole or in part, across organizations in every industry sector.

We have retained the same definitions as in the PMI (2007) standard as follows:

- *Competence:* "A cluster of related knowledge, attitudes, skills, and other personal characteristics that affects a major part of one's job (i.e., one or more key roles or responsibilities), correlates with performance on the job, can be measured against well-accepted standards, and can be improved by means of training and development" (p. 73).

- *Knowledge:* "Knowing something with the familiarity gained through experience, education, observation, or investigation. It is understanding a process, practice, or technique, or how to use a tool" (p. 74).
- *Skill:* "Ability to use knowledge, a developed aptitude, and/or a capability to effectively and readily execute or perform an activity" (p. 75).

Following the PMI (2007) project manager competency format, we also used the convention of identifying *performance* competencies as well as *personal* competencies. By using both sets of competencies, program managers, prospective program managers, and their organizations can identify any gaps that may exist and determine how best to fill them. Individuals can use the model to help them further improve their overall effectiveness as a program manager or to determine whether or not program management is a desired career path. Organizations can use the model, tailoring it as required, to meet their unique needs to best match individuals to open positions as new programs are undertaken, existing program managers leave to take on other assignments, or as existing programs are reprioritized.

Model Overview

The Levin-Ward Program Management Competency Model consists of six performance competencies and eight personal competencies that are applied when performing program management. Figure 2.1 provides a graphical depiction of the model.

Following is a description of each of the competencies represented.

Performance Competencies

These competencies are ones that state what the program manager should do by applying his or her knowledge of program management

Figure 2.1   The Levin-Ward program management competency model.

in order to be able to deliver the proposed and planned benefits of the program. These competencies are aligned with the six domains of program management:

1. *Defining the program:* includes activities such as defining the program objectives and requirements, creating a high-level roadmap, preparing a benefits realization plan, conducting an initial stakeholder analysis, validating the program's priority and alignment to strategic objectives, preparing a business case, and obtaining the required authorization to proceed.

2. *Initiating the program:* includes activities such as articulating the program mission statement, developing the high-level program WBS and milestone plan, developing an accountability matrix, establishing project management standards for the component projects, defining measurement criteria,

obtaining senior management approval for the program charter, and conducting a program kickoff meeting.

3. *Planning the program:* includes activities such as developing a detailed program scope statement and Program Work Breakdown Structure (PWBS), establishing the program management plan and baseline, reviewing and leveling resource requirements to optimize the program plan, defining the program management information system (PMIS), and developing the transition plan.

4. *Executing the program:* includes activities such as implementing the program management plan and all subsidiary plans, consolidating project and program data to monitor program performance, chartering component projects as necessary, continuously motivating team members through various activities, deploying uniform standards across all projects, capturing program status and disseminating information to key stakeholders, and closing component projects as necessary.

5. *Monitoring and controlling the program:* includes activities such as analyzing cost, schedule, and quality variances to the program plan and making decisions to correct deficiencies or promote continued above par performance; forecasting project and program outcomes by gathering relevant data and identifying trends; ensuring stated benefits are being realized or will be realized as a result of execution, and managing change in accordance with the change management plan.

6. *Closing the program:* includes activities such as completing a program performance analysis report, executing the transition plan, conducting stakeholder review meetings, ensuring the official closeout of all contracts and agreements, and documenting lessons learned.

Table 2.2 identifies the performance competencies for each of the program management domains listed above.

Each of the elements of performance competence for program managers then are expanded to show performance criteria and the types of evidence required to see if these criteria are met. Table 2.3 provides an abbreviated example.

Table 2.2   Performance Competencies According to Program Domains

---

1.0 DEFINING THE PROGRAM
 1. Strategic benefits of the program are understood by all stakeholders
 2. A plan to initiate the program is prepared
 3. The program's objectives are aligned with the strategic goals of the organization
 4. A high-level business case is developed for the program
 5. A number of stage gates or check points are identified when program status (including benefits realization) will be reviewed

2.0 INITIATING THE PROGRAM
 1. A program charter is prepared
 2. The program vision is documented to describe the end state and its benefits to the organization
 3. Key program decision makers are identified
 4. Stakeholders' expectations and interests are identified
 5. High-level risks to the program are identified
 6. Candidate projects to be in the program, as well as non-project work, are identified
 7. An initial infrastructure for program management is determined
 8. The timetable to complete the program is determined
 9. Initial estimates of the program's cost are prepared
10. Key resources for program management are identified to set up the program
11. The program charter is approved

3.0 PLANNING THE PROGRAM
 1. A program management plan is prepared
 2. A benefits realization plan is prepared
 3. Key program risks and issues are identified
 4. The program's budget is determined
 5. Dependencies, constraints, and assumptions are documented
 6. A strategy to manage the program and its components is agreed upon and documented
 7. Necessary feasibility studies are conducted
 8. A roadmap or architecture showing the interrelationships among the component projects and non-project work in the program is prepared
 9. A communications strategy for each key stakeholder is determined
10. A Program Management Office (PMO) is approved and implemented
11. Tools, processes, and techniques required for program management are obtained
12. The program management plan is approved and implemented
13. A program management governance structure is determined
14. A program control framework is established to assist in benefits measurement as well as in overall management of the program's components

Table 2.2   Performance Competencies According to Program Domains (Continued)

4.0 EXECUTING THE PROGRAM

  1. Projects are initiated as part of the program

  2. Shared resources required for component projects and the non-project work are coordinated

  3. Change requests are reviewed

  4. Additional work is authorized as required

  5. Communication with stakeholders is fostered and encouraged at all levels

  6. Communication with members of the Program Governance* Board occurs on a regular basis

  7. Alignment of the program's goals and benefits is assessed against that of the organization

  8. Common activities among the program's projects and non-project work are coordinated

  9. Dependencies with other organizational initiatives are coordinated

10. The program management plan is executed

5.0 MONITORING AND CONTROLLING THE PROGRAM

  1. Progress is analyzed according to the program management plan

  2. Benefits realization is analyzed according to the benefits realization plan

  3. Issues and risks are continuously identified, and corrective actions are taken as required

  4. External environmental changes are analyzed to determine possible impact on the program and its realization of benefits

  5. Governance oversight is regularly practiced at the program and project levels

  6. Program changes are implemented in accordance with established integrated change control procedures

  7. Program execution is monitored according to the program management plan

  8. Schedule slippages and opportunities are identified and managed

  9. Proactive cost control is practiced

10. Stakeholder expectations are managed

11. Performance data are consolidated to determine appropriate resource use to deliver benefits

12. Components transition to closure

6.0 CLOSING THE PROGRAM

  1. The program is formally closed

  2. Products and services transition to operations

  3. Program benefits are realized

  4. Customer support is provided (as applicable, such as defined in a contract)

  5. Lessons learned are integrated into the organization's knowledge management system

  6. Feedback is provided on areas outside the scope of the program

  7. Program documents are archived for reuse

  8. Contractual obligations are met

  9. Intellectual property is captured for reuse

10. A legacy of benefits sustainment is achieved

* This could also be called a Steering Committee, Oversight Committee, or similar name. There are probably as many names for these types of "boards" as there are organizations.

Table 2.3   Example of Evidence for One Performance Competency

ELEMENT 3.2 A BENEFITS REALIZATION PLAN IS PREPARED

PERFORMANCE CRITERIA	TYPES OF EVIDENCE
Identifies the program's benefits	Documented benefits, both tangible and intangible
Defines the program's benefits in measureable outcomes	Documented benefits that are specific, measurable, attainable, realistic, and time based
States roles and responsibilities for benefits realization and management	Documented roles and responsibilities in a Responsibility Assignment Matrix (RAM) or in a Responsible, Accountable, Consult, Inform (RACI) chart

Following the PMI (2007) guidance at the project level, the purpose of these units of performance competence is to highlight what is required by program managers in most programs most of the time. The authors do not suggest that these units of performance are exhaustive and can be applied to all programs all the time. Each program manager must decide which performance criteria are relevant to his or her program. However, we believe these can act as a guide to help get started. Each competency described in Table 2.2 is supported by evidence as shown in Table 2.3 in the model. Similar to units of performance competencies, the examples of the evidence provided in the Levin-Ward model are just that—"examples." The list is neither exhaustive nor exclusive. In any program, there may be more or less, and it is up to the program manager to determine the best evidence to provide as it relates to each unit of performance competence.

Personal Competencies

The personal competencies relate to the interpersonal skills to enhance the program manager's abilities to successfully "perform," or execute, the performance competencies. We based these competencies on the GAO (2005) study, our survey of PgMPs, and the program manager knowledge and skills discussed in PMI (2008d). These personal competencies are grouped into eight areas:

1. *Communicating:* Project management research has shown that an effective project manager communicates approximately 90% of his or her time. In program management, communications consumes an even greater amount of time as there are more diverse stakeholders and more stakeholders who are external to the organization. Active listening is included in this category. The PMI (2008d) states that communicating is the most important competency.

2. *Leading:* Although the vision or end state of the program is set forth in the initial business case, the program manager is responsible for ensuring that this vision is understood at all levels of involvement in the program. Leadership involves setting forth this vision and establishing the program's direction. Because the program consists of projects and non-project work, it also involves identifying interdependencies between them and making decisions as required. Project managers, for example, will escalate issues and risks to the program manager requiring him or her to make decisions, sometimes quickly; or on others, they may need to escalate these issues and risks to the Program Governance Board for advice and decisions.

3. *Building relationships:* In program management, stakeholder management is a knowledge area (PMI, 2008d). The program manager is responsible not only for identifying those stakeholders who may influence or impact his or her program, but also for formulating a stakeholder management strategy to engage them throughout the program's life cycle, and then memorializing that strategy in a stakeholder management plan. The specific interests of each stakeholder must be noted and respected, and dealing with the various stakeholder groups requires significant time and effort by the program manager and his or her team.

4. *Negotiating:* The large number of stakeholders typically involved with a program means that there is a need for the program manager to have the highest level of negotiation skills and competencies. These important skills will be applied to such situations as negotiating for resources, making sure the program remains a top priority in the organization's portfolio,

convincing the Program Governance Board to make certain decisions when undergoing a stage gate review, and encouraging and promoting stakeholder support.

5. *Thinking critically:* A critical thinker is one who has the ability to identify the important questions to ask and problems to solve in a way that defines them clearly. Following identification of the issue, the relevant facts and information are gathered and analyzed in a logical or even an abstract manner. Based on the interpretation of the facts at hand, the person then comes to well-reasoned conclusions or solutions that are then tested against relevant criteria. Critical thinkers have the ability to think openly, to not be influenced by others' thinking, and to identify the assumptions, constraints, and implications and consequences of their decisions. Thinking critically also means communicating effectively with others in formulating solutions to complex problems. It is, in short, the ability to think about one's thinking, while one is thinking, to improve one's thinking. Better thinking typically yields better results. The program manager addressing complex programs is well served by a competency that promotes more insightful analysis of the problems and opportunities at hand. Given the nature of the interdependencies of complex programs, the ability to "connect the dots" and understand the integrative nature of such endeavors is crucial to managing and controlling such efforts.

6. *Facilitating:* It is not the program manager's job to do all the work of the program; that is the responsibility of the project managers, operations managers, and the team. That said, the program manager must set the stage for success by creating an environment in which people can perform their assigned tasks without extensive roadblocks. If there are issues that require resolution, or risks in which the planned response is not effective, these must be escalated to the program manager so he or she can assist the project manager or team member as quickly as possible. This facilitation role is also significant if issues or risks must be escalated to higher levels such as to the Program Governance Board. To be sure, if the priorities

of the program change, the program manager must communicate these changes to affected parties. Additionally, the program manager is responsible for ensuring that the team's policies, procedures, and processes are conducive to, and will help the team realize, the stated program benefits.

7. *Mentoring:* Most programs last a number of years; as such, the program manager can expect staff turnover throughout its life cycle. The program managers, and others in the organization, need to serve as mentors to team members so they (the mentors) can assume additional responsibilities and advance to positions of greater responsibility as the need demands. This mentoring function is one that requires support and commitment by the program manager, as well as by the person being mentored. As such, well-defined goals and objectives for the mentoring relationship must be established. A formal documented commitment by each party to the mentoring initiative is required. On a large program, it may be desirable for the program manager to set up a mentoring program at a variety of levels. For greater objectivity and confidentiality, it may very well be more effective if the mentor is someone who is familiar with the program but lacks direct involvement in it.

8. *Embracing change:* Unlike the project manager who generally strives to keep changes to his or her project to a minimum, the program manager recognizes that changes are going to occur on the program, and that they can be positive. He or she therefore must keep an open mind to, and embrace, change, which will have a positive effect on program objectives. Additionally, the program manager must realize that change may come from internal initiatives or external factors. A change on one project, while at first may be perceived as negative, may in fact be a benefit to other projects or other work under way on the program. Given the longer life of most programs than projects, technology changes also may be beneficial.

In our model, these eight competencies are described in a similar manner to the performance competencies (Table 2.4).

Table 2.4   Program Manager Personal Competencies

PERSONAL COMPETENCIES

1.0 Communicating
1. Actively listens, understands, and responds to stakeholders
2. Uses the key channels of communications
3. Ensures the quality of the information that is communicated
4. Tailors the information to the audience
5. Effectively uses each of the different communications dimensions

2.0 Leading
1. Implements the program's vision
2. Establishes the program's direction
3. Recognizes the interdependencies within the program
4. Takes calculated risks; is venturesome
5. Assumes ownership of the program

3.0 Building Relationships
1. Builds trust among stakeholders, clients, and team members
2. Leverages the organization's political dynamics to promote program goals
3. Advocates for diversity and treats others with courtesy and respect
4. Establishes and demonstrates high standards for personal and team member performance
5. Promotes and demonstrates ethics, integrity, and adherence to corporate values in all interactions

4.0 Negotiating
1. Obtains needed program resources
2. Ensures program alignment with the organization's strategies
3. Works proactively with the Program Governance Board
4. Promotes overall stakeholder support

5.0 Thinking Critically
1. Conducts ongoing analyses to identify trends, variances, and issues
2. Applies fact-based decision making to current and prospective issues
3. Works proactively with the Program Governance Structure that provides for decision making at the appropriate levels
4. Constructively challenges common beliefs and assumptions—always looking for a better way

6.0 Facilitating
1. Plans for success from the start of the program
2. Ensures that all team members work together to achieve program goals
3. Effectively resolves issues to solve problems
4. Effectively handles personal and team adversity

Table 2.4   Program Manager Personal Competencies (Continued)

7.0 Mentoring

1. Supports mentoring for program team members
2. Establishes a formal mentoring program
3. Supports individual and team development activities
4. Recognizes and rewards individual and team accomplishments

8.0 Embracing Change

1. Establishes an environment receptive to change
2. Influences factors that may result in change
3. Plans for change and its potential impact
4. Manages changes when they do occur

Table 2.5   Example of Evidence for One Personal Competency

ELEMENT 7.4 RECOGNIZES AND REWARDS INDIVIDUAL AND TEAM ACCOMPLISHMENTS

PERFORMANCE CRITERIA	TYPES OF EVIDENCE
Celebrates success throughout the program	Examples include: Formal recognition of accomplishments by specific individuals and the entire team How the team celebrated achievements

Each of the above elements of personal competence for program managers are expanded to show performance criteria and the types of evidence required to see if these criteria are met. Table 2.5 provides an abbreviated example.

The authors do not suggest that these units of performance are exhaustive and can be applied to all programs all the time. Each program manager must decide which performance criteria are relevant to his or her program. However, we believe these criteria can act as a guide to help get started. Each competency described in Table 2.4 is supported by evidence as shown in Table 2.5 in the model. Similar to units of performance competencies, the examples of the evidence provided in the Levin-Ward model are just that—"examples." The list is neither exhaustive nor exclusive. In any program, there may be more or less, and it is up to the program manager to determine the best evidence to provide as it relates to each unit of performance competence.

Model Validation

After completion of the decomposition of each performance and personal competency element into specific criteria and evidence, the authors validated the model by presenting it to a subset of PgMPs whom the authors contacted to gather competency characteristics.

3

THE MODEL

Performance Competencies

Using the six program management domains, each of the performance competencies is described here based on each element in Chapter 2. Performance criteria are specified for each element, along with the types of evidence to gather to support it and ensure it is in place.

1.0 Defining the Program	
JUSTIFYING AND PRIORITIZING THE IMPORTANCE OF THE PROGRAM	
ELEMENT 1.1 STRATEGIC BENEFITS OF THE PROGRAM ARE UNDERSTOOD BY ALL STAKEHOLDERS	
PERFORMANCE CRITERIA	TYPES OF EVIDENCE
1. Identifies, qualifies, and quantifies the business benefits	Documented evidence that high-level benefits have been identified
2. Analyzes expected benefits	Documented evidence enumerating the information the program's stakeholders will receive Example: The strategic directive
ELEMENT 1.2 A PLAN TO INITIATE THE PROGRAM IS PREPARED	
PERFORMANCE CRITERIA	TYPES OF EVIDENCE
1. Analyzes the key stakeholders and strategy area to be addressed	Stakeholder analysis document
2. Develops a high-level plan	High-level plan showing the stimuli that triggered the program, the objectives, and how objectives align with those of the organization
3. Follows principles of organizational change management	Documents showing the organizational change approach to be used

ELEMENT 1.3 *THE PROGRAM'S OBJECTIVES ARE ALIGNED WITH THE STRATEGIC GOALS OF THE ORGANIZATION*	
PERFORMANCE CRITERIA	TYPES OF EVIDENCE
1. Follows the organization's selection process for programs and projects	Documents showing— • the program's strategic objectives and benefits • that the objectives are best realized if a program is established
2. Assesses organizational and business strategies	Documents showing the alignment of the program with the organization's strategic goals
3. Uses the strategic directive	Example: The organization's strategic objective for the concept, vision, and mission for the program
4. Describes high-level program goals to key stakeholders	Example: The strategic directive

ELEMENT 1.4 *A HIGH-LEVEL BUSINESS CASE IS DEVELOPED FOR THE PROGRAM*	
PERFORMANCE CRITERIA	TYPES OF EVIDENCE
1. Develops a high-level business case	Documents showing the needs, costs, benefits, feasibility, and justification for the program
2. Justifies the effort to assess the program's costs and benefits	Example: The business case
3. Determines program parameters and constraints	Documents showing the parameters used to assess objectives and constraints for the program Example: A list of parameters in the business case
4. Determines whether existing projects or other components will be part of the program	Example: The business case, noting expected program benefits

ELEMENT 1.5 *A NUMBER OF STAGE GATES OR CHECK POINTS ARE IDENTIFIED WHEN PROGRAM STATUS (INCLUDING BENEFITS REALIZATION) WILL BE REVIEWED*	
PERFORMANCE CRITERIA	TYPES OF EVIDENCE
1. Determines how governance will be practiced in the program	Document showing— • the existing governance structure in the organization • a proposed program governance structure • how program reviews will be conducted as part of a portfolio management process at the organizational level
2. Establishes check points to be used throughout the program	Document showing how stage gates will be used to ensure that the program is on track
3. Begins the program initiation phase	Document showing that the program has passed the first stage gate and can be initiated

2.0 Initiating the Program

DEVELOPING IN MORE DETAIL HOW THE PROGRAM WILL BE SET UP AND MANAGED

ELEMENT 2.1 A PROGRAM CHARTER IS PREPARED

PERFORMANCE CRITERIA	TYPES OF EVIDENCE
1. Consolidates existing information about the program	Example: An initial draft of the program charter
2. Prepares the information to begin program charter	Example: The program charter; its approval will lead to the Set-Up phase in the life cycle
3. Identifies program constraints	A documented list of constraints Example: The business case for the program

ELEMENT 2.2   THE PROGRAM VISION IS DOCUMENTED TO DESCRIBE THE END STATE AND ITS BENEFIT TO THE ORGANIZATION

PERFORMANCE CRITERIA	TYPES OF EVIDENCE
1. Determines the end state of the program	Example: The program charter, which will include a description of the end state
2. Establishes a process to define the program's benefits or expectations	Example: An enumeration of the high-level benefits to be achieved
3. Determines the program's feasibility and ensures it is agreed to by key stakeholders	Example: The program charter, which includes benefits, objectives, and critical success factors to achieve
4. Determines how the program links to the organization's ongoing work and strategic objectives	Documents showing— • the program's objectives and how they link to those of the organization's strategic objectives in the charter • the extent to which the program meets organizational needs
5. Uses the strategic directive	Documents showing — • the organization's concept, vision, and mission for the program • high-level program goals
6. Prepares a "what if" analysis	Documents showing results of a comparative advantage analysis to see if strategic directives and intended benefits might be achieved in other ways

ELEMENT 2.3 KEY PROGRAM DECISION MAKERS ARE IDENTIFIED

PERFORMANCE CRITERIA	TYPES OF EVIDENCE
1. Identifies potential members of the Program Governance Board	Documents showing— • official appointment of the executive sponsor • official appointment of the program manager
2. Determines whether a preliminary pilot program may be warranted	Documents showing the decision regarding the need for a pilot

ELEMENT 2.4 STAKEHOLDERS' EXPECTATIONS AND INTERESTS ARE IDENTIFIED	
PERFORMANCE CRITERIA	TYPES OF EVIDENCE
1. Identifies all stakeholders noting the most important ones	Example: A list of key stakeholders and their probable attitudes toward the program
2. Prepares an initial strategy to manage each stakeholder	Documents showing an initial stakeholder management strategy that depicts potential expectations of probable stakeholders
3. Obtains formal acceptance of the program's concept and approach from key stakeholders	Documented sign-off by key stakeholders showing that the program can achieve strategic benefits
4. Communicates the overall scope of the program	Examples include: The program roadmap The program communications plan

ELEMENT 2.5 HIGH-LEVEL RISKS TO THE PROGRAM ARE IDENTIFIED	
PERFORMANCE CRITERIA	TYPES OF EVIDENCE
1. Prepares a list of high-level known program risks and issues	Documents showing— • risks and issues known during initiation • the most critical risks whose impact may significantly affect achievement of program objectives Example: The business case for the program
2. Analyzes risks with any existing projects that will be part of the program	Example: The risk registers for these extant projects
3. Analyzes strengths, weaknesses, opportunities, and threats	Documents showing the results of a strengths, weaknesses, opportunities, and threats (SWOT) analysis

ELEMENT 2.6 CANDIDATE PROJECTS TO BE IN THE PROGRAM, AS WELL AS NON-PROJECT WORK, ARE IDENTIFIED	
PERFORMANCE CRITERIA	TYPES OF EVIDENCE
1. Determines criteria to group proposed or existing projects and non-project work into the program	Documents identifying candidate projects and other work to be included in the program, including the benefits from grouping them into a program
2. Develops an initial program roadmap	Example: A roadmap at a high level describing the program's intended direction

ELEMENT 2.7 AN INITIAL INFRASTRUCTURE FOR PROGRAM MANAGEMENT IS DETERMINED	
PERFORMANCE CRITERIA	TYPES OF EVIDENCE
1. Determines what type of infrastructure is required to manage the program	Documents showing the management infrastructure needed for a new organization to plan, develop, and manage the program
2. Provides a high-level view of the program's infrastructure	Example: The program roadmap and program organization chart

ELEMENT 2.8 THE TIMETABLE TO COMPLETE THE PROGRAM IS DETERMINED	
PERFORMANCE CRITERIA	TYPES OF EVIDENCE
1. Prepares an order-of-magnitude estimate of the time required to complete the program	Example: A high-level integrated schedule of all program components

ELEMENT 2.9 INITIAL ESTIMATES OF THE PROGRAM'S COST ARE PREPARED	
PERFORMANCE CRITERIA	TYPES OF EVIDENCE
1. Prepares an order-of-magnitude estimate of the budget requirements	Example: An initial cost estimate
2. Determines funding goals	Documents showing— • the funding goals for the program (e.g., business case updates or program financial framework) • funding constraints
3. Prepares financial analyses	Documents showing results of the identification of sources and schedules of funding
4. Obtains funding to initiate the program	Example: Funds available according to identified program milestones Documents showing ways to obtain funds to bridge the gap between paying out monies to develop and obtain the program benefits
5. Identifies the overall financial framework	Documents showing— • the program's financial framework to show how it will be financed • updates to the business case • the type of program and the funding structure
6. Prepares a cost/benefit analysis	Documents showing the financial and nonfinancial results to define benefits and compare them to costs
7. Establishes payment schedules	Documents showing milestones when payments to contractors are required
8. Determines funding methods	Documents showing factors that affect different methods of program funding

ELEMENT 2.10 KEY RESOURCES FOR PROGRAM MANAGEMENT ARE IDENTIFIED TO SET UP THE PROGRAM	
PERFORMANCE CRITERIA	TYPES OF EVIDENCE
1. Prepares an order-of-magnitude estimate of needed resources	Example: A list of resources (personnel, materials, etc.) required for the initial stages of the program
2. Uses the strategic directive	Documents showing the core resources and desired competencies required for the program team
3. Analyzes existing programs and other work under way in the organization in terms of available resources	Documents showing the results of analyses performed, noting where resources may be used for the program

ELEMENT 2.11 THE PROGRAM CHARTER IS APPROVED	
PERFORMANCE CRITERIA	TYPES OF EVIDENCE
1. Receives approval from the Program Governance Board to begin planning the program	Documents showing sign-offs of the charter's approval; if not approved, document showing why the program was not approved
2. Receives authorization to use resources according to stated guidelines	Example: The charter providing guidelines as to how to use organizational resources
3. Assigns the program manager	Documents showing the program manager's roles and responsibilities, and delegation of authority to apply resources to the program
4. Revises the business case (as necessary)	Example: Updated business case, to include any information regarding approval or disapproval of program charter

3.0 Planning the Program	
POSITIONING THE PROGRAM FOR SUCCESSFUL EXECUTION	
ELEMENT 3.1 A PROGRAM MANAGEMENT PLAN IS PREPARED	
PERFORMANCE CRITERIA	TYPES OF EVIDENCE
1. Develops a program management plan	Documents showing— • the plan for the program • key elements of program direction and management • how decisions are to be presented and recorded • how performance reports are prepared and distributed
2. Prepares a Program Work Breakdown Structure (PWBS)	Example: A PWBS to formalize the program scope
3. Prepares a program master schedule for the program	Example: A schedule showing the timeline for milestones and deliverables
4. Determines how quality will be planned	Example: A quality management plan describing the program's quality management approaches and activities in quality assurance and quality control
5. Prepares a program transition plan	Documents showing how to move from the development stage to an operational stage when the program has delivered its benefits
6. Integrates the subsidiary plans for the program	Documents showing the various plans that are part of the program management plan
ELEMENT 3.2 A BENEFITS REALIZATION PLAN IS PREPARED	
PERFORMANCE CRITERIA	TYPES OF EVIDENCE
1. Develops a benefits realization plan	Documents showing how the program's benefits will be realized Example: Metrics to use to track progress in benefits delivery
2. Assesses the program's outputs/ deliverables	Documents showing links of the desired outputs/ deliverables to the planned program outcomes
3. Performs benefits analysis	Documents showing those benefits that have been achieved on an ongoing basis
4. Identifies processes and resources needed for transition of program's products and service to the organization	Example: The program transition plan
5. Describes the high-level requirements needed to deliver program benefits	Documents showing program requirements
6. Establishes program financial metrics	Documents showing how program benefits are measured and are linked to expenditures

ELEMENT 3.3 KEY PROGRAM RISKS AND ISSUES ARE IDENTIFIED	
PERFORMANCE CRITERIA	TYPES OF EVIDENCE
1. Identifies and analyzes risk and plans program risk responses	Example: The risks listed in the scope statement Documents showing— • risk categories • identification and analysis approaches used Example: Program risk register
2. Defines risk profiles	Documents showing— • risk profiles of the organization to help manage program risks • stakeholder tolerances for risk
3. Conducts risk planning meetings	Documents showing results and action items as these meetings are held
4. Prepares a program risk management plan	Example: The program's risk management plan
5. Identifies the interdependencies between component risks	Documents showing— • approaches that will be used to integrate program component risks in the life cycle • factors that will provide an environment to support risk management of program components
6. Establishes contingency reserves for identified contingency plans	Documents showing the existence of reserves for risk responses noted in the risk register
7. Establishes a management reserve for risks that are unknown and unknowable	Documents showing the existence of a management reserve in the program's budget
8. Establishes an issue escalation process	Documents showing methods to track issues and resolve them at the program level and inter-component level, and when to escalate them to the sponsor or the Program Governance Board
ELEMENT 3.4 THE PROGRAM'S BUDGET IS DETERMINED	
PERFORMANCE CRITERIA	TYPES OF EVIDENCE
1. Prepares a budget for the program	Documents showing the initial program budget plus overhead Examples include: Program budget baseline Payment schedules at the program level Payment schedules at the component level
2. Performs cash flow analysis	Example: The program's funding schedule
3. Determines funding goals	Documents showing the program's funding goals
4. Prepares a program financial framework	Documents showing— • a plan to define and describe program funding flows • the needed changes to the business case
5. Prepares a program financial plan	Example: The program financial plan

6. Establishes program payment schedules	Documents showing a schedule and milestones when funding is received
7. Identifies program operational costs	Documents showing operational and infrastructure program costs
8. Determines the total cost of ownership	Documents showing use of value analysis or value engineering to minimize the total cost of ownership
9. Prepares a program cost estimate	Example: An overall cost estimate for the total program

ELEMENT 3.5 DEPENDENCIES, CONSTRAINTS, AND ASSUMPTIONS ARE DOCUMENTED

PERFORMANCE CRITERIA	TYPES OF EVIDENCE
1. Identifies assumptions and constraints	Example: Program assumptions and constraints are included in the scope statement
2. Identifies the program's boundaries	Example: Boundaries are defined in the scope statement
3. Performs capacity planning	Documents showing resource availability and limitations Example: A program resource plan
4. Determines schedule constraints	Documents showing the program's schedule constraints in the program master schedule Example: Component milestones to indicate internal program dependencies
5. Determines communications constraints and assumptions	Documents showing constraints and assumptions in communications planning
6. Determines funding constraints	Documents showing the funding constraints affecting the program

ELEMENT 3.6 A STRATEGY TO MANAGE THE PROGRAM AND ITS COMPONENTS IS AGREED UPON AND DOCUMENTED

PERFORMANCE CRITERIA	TYPES OF EVIDENCE
1. Prepares a process for customer acceptance reviews for each deliverable	Examples include: Relevant testing and inspection techniques and the results of such reviews Ways to improve deliverables to meet requirements
2. Prepares a strategy to mitigate customer dissatisfaction	Documents showing an approach to assess customer acceptance issues early in the process
3. Uses design reviews to ensure compliance to best practices	Documents showing the results of various design reviews held during the program
4. Decomposes high-level program requirements for components	Example: Component requirements documents
5. Identifies relationships among components	Documents showing the structure of the program's components Example: A program architecture baseline
6. Uses the PWBS for control and communication with managers of component projects	Documents showing the WBS of program components Example: The PWBS

7. Determines the need for program procurements	Example: The program procurement management plan showing the results of make-or-buy analyses
8. Prepares a plan to administer contracts	Example: The contract/vendor management plan
9. Prepares criteria for component initiation	Documents showing component initiation criteria

ELEMENT 3.7 NECESSARY FEASIBILITY STUDIES ARE CONDUCTED	
PERFORMANCE CRITERIA	TYPES OF EVIDENCE
1. Assesses market environmental factors	Documents showing— • environmental factors affecting the program • factors that could affect procurements • environmental factors that may lead to significant financial impacts on the original business case • financing options for contractors and subcontractors
2. Conducts benchmarking to generate ideas for improvement and provide certain measurement criteria for performance	Documents benchmarking studies

ELEMENT 3.8 A ROADMAP OR ARCHITECTURE SHOWING THE INTERRELATIONSHIPS AMONG THE COMPONENT PROJECTS AND NON-PROJECT WORK IN THE PROGRAM IS PREPARED	
PERFORMANCE CRITERIA	TYPES OF EVIDENCE
1. Describes program's vision	Example: A scope statement to define the vision Documents about the broad outcomes expected of the program
2. Evaluates program management best practices and applies those as required	Example: The use of a best practice library
3. Updates the program roadmap	Example: The program roadmap, using a rolling wave approach with more details as the program ensues

ELEMENT 3.9 A COMMUNICATIONS STRATEGY FOR EACH KEY STAKEHOLDER IS DETERMINED	
PERFORMANCE CRITERIA	TYPES OF EVIDENCE
1. Establishes a strategy for stakeholder communications	Documents showing— • the key stakeholders on the program—both internal and external • each stakeholder's communications requirements • the results of a communications requirements analysis Examples include: • A stakeholder management plan • A stakeholder register • A communications strategy
2. Uses the scope statement for stakeholder acceptance criteria	Documents showing stakeholder sign-off on deliverables and benefits

3. Communicates planned outcomes to all stakeholders	Documents showing— • stakeholder preferences • communications factors affecting the program Examples include: The communications management plan A communications log Results of interviews with stakeholders Results from focus groups
4. Reviews the organization's communications strategy	Documents showing results to make sure the program's strategy supports that of the organization
5. Uses a variety of methods to identify program stakeholders	Documents showing— • Stakeholder register • Stakeholder Inventory • Stakeholder management strategy • Program stakeholder management plan

ELEMENT 3.10 A PROGRAM MANAGEMENT OFFICE (PMO) IS APPROVED AND IMPLEMENTED

PERFORMANCE CRITERIA	TYPES OF EVIDENCE
1. Obtains approval to set up a PMO	Example: A charter for the PMO
2. Identifies program management artifacts for use by the PMO	Example: The PWBS Documents showing items from a best practice library
3. Uses organizational policies and guidelines	Example: Program-level processes that do not conflict with organizational processes
4. Shares and optimizes scarce resources	Documents showing resource allocation approaches used
5. Structures the PMO to address reporting and governance requirements	Documents showing the reports prepared and distributed
6. Uses the PMO to prepare and coordinate assessments of change requests	Documents showing the results of change request assessments
7. Uses the PMO to support tracking of risks and issues	Example: Risk and issue logs
8. Uses the PMO to assist in managing contracts and procurements	Documents showing— • the specific requirements of each procurement on the program • the unique terms and conditions for each program contract
9. Uses the PMO to implement the program management methodology	Documents showing the organization's program management methodology as tailored for the program
10. Uses the PMO to ensure each project is using the same project management methodology	Documents showing each component project is using the same project management methodology for consistency and reporting purpose
11. Uses the PMO to manage the program management information system (PMIS)	Example: The tools and processes in the PMIS

ELEMENT 3.11 TOOLS, PROCESSES, AND TECHNIQUES REQUIRED FOR PROGRAM MANAGEMENT ARE OBTAINED	
PERFORMANCE CRITERIA	TYPES OF EVIDENCE
1. Acquires needed processes and systems for program support	Examples include: The benefits realization plan, which lists what is required for ultimate transition The program management methodology
2. Uses a variety of methods to gather requirements	Documents showing the results of interviews with stakeholders, focus groups, brainstorming sessions, and questionnaires and surveys
3. Prepares a task responsibility matrix	Example: A matrix showing roles and responsibilities and the level of involvement of team members
4. Obtains system configuration tools	Example: A document repository and version control tools
5. Establishes a program management information system (PMIS) to manage program data and information	Example: The PMIS Documents showing how to communicate status, changes, and performance
6. Uses a variety of planning techniques	Documents showing techniques for planning the schedule, program finances and budget, required resources, risks, quality standards, and procurement requirements
7. Acquires a program scheduling tool that provides high-level program timelines, plus individual project-level plans	Examples include: The schedule that first is high level and later is updated, showing component milestones that are an output of the program or have an interdependency with another component The timing of program packages for forecasts of completion dates A schedule management plan
8. Provides contractors access to tools and other resources as required	Documents showing contractors using technology-compatible tools with those of the program team
9. Uses a variety of tools and techniques to identify potential suppliers	Documents showing approaches used to identify suppliers Example: A qualified seller list
ELEMENT 3.12 THE PROGRAM MANAGEMENT PLAN IS APPROVED	
PERFORMANCE CRITERIA	TYPES OF EVIDENCE
1. Obtains approval of the plan	Documents showing sign-offs by the sponsor, key stakeholders, and members of the Program Governance Board

ELEMENT 3.13 A PROGRAM MANAGEMENT GOVERNANCE STRUCTURE IS DETERMINED	
PERFORMANCE CRITERIA	TYPES OF EVIDENCE
1. Determines key governance roles and responsibilities	Documents showing roles and responsibilities for program governance Example: A program governance plan
2. Determines program governance goals	Example: A program governance plan
3. Conducts periodic health checks	Documents showing action items and minutes of program performance and status reviews by the Program Governance Board
4. Holds program-level review meetings at defined stage gates	Documents showing action items and minutes of discussions of individual project reports with the Program Governance Board in terms of overall program progress
5. Approves the program management methodology to be followed	Documents showing the existence of the methodology at the organizational level
6. Determines objectives and timing of program audits	Example: The program audit plan

ELEMENT 3.14 A PROGRAM CONTROL FRAMEWORK IS ESTABLISHED TO ASSIST IN BENEFITS MEASUREMENT AS WELL AS IN OVERALL MANAGEMENT OF THE PROGRAM'S COMPONENTS	
PERFORMANCE CRITERIA	TYPES OF EVIDENCE
1. Prepares a program scope statement	Example: A scope statement as the basis for future program decisions to manage scope throughout the program Documents showing the product scope
2. Establishes a process to manage all stages of the program to satisfy the use of the program's outputs	Documents showing— • the use of the program's outputs, included as part of the benefits realization plan • that outcomes are achieved as part of the benefits realization plan before formal closure
3. Uses a program management methodology	Documents showing practices, techniques, procedures, and guidelines for managing the program
4. Sets defined limits for various levels of authority and responsibility	Documents showing delegation of authority levels of project and operations managers, the program manager, and the Program Governance Board concerning cost, quality, schedule, scope, issues, or risks

4.0 Executing the Program	
PERFORMING THE WORK ACCORDING TO THE PROGRAM MANAGEMENT PLAN	
ELEMENT 4.1 PROJECTS ARE INITIATED AS PART OF THE PROGRAM	
PERFORMANCE CRITERIA	TYPES OF EVIDENCE
1. Initiates and terminates projects and non-project work with the program	Documents showing the strategic direction and business case Example: The program roadmap to show timing of components Documents showing— • requests to initiate a component • requests to terminate a component Example: A governance structure to monitor and track benefits delivery and progress of projects in the program and non-project work
2. Facilitates and resolves inter-project issues, risks, and constraints	Examples include: A risk register An issue register Documents showing how any constraints were handled
3. Assesses change requests	Documents showing— • the impact analysis of the change requesl • the change requests escalated to the Program Governance Board and the results • updates to the program roadmap
4. Executes the program management plan	Documents showing— • updates to the program management plan • progress and completion of deliverables Example: A decision log
5. Executes the procurement management plan	Example: Procurement management status reports indicating progress on plan elements
6. Executes the contract management plan	Documents showing engagement and management of suppliers for such activities as quality assurance, acceptance of deliverables, and receipt and payment of invoices Example: A payment control system Documents showing— • the results of contract performance reviews • the results of inspections and procurement audits
7. Updates the budget allocations	Documents showing updates to the program budget allocations affecting the different components in the program management plan

ELEMENT 4.2 SHARED RESOURCES REQUIRED FOR COMPONENT PROJECTS AND THE NON-PROJECT WORK ARE COORDINATED	
PERFORMANCE CRITERIA	TYPES OF EVIDENCE
1. Monitors program-level resource use	Documents showing— • reallocation of resources as required • compliance with the Human Resources/Talent Management Personnel guidelines • updates to the program resource plan Example: Activities of the PMO staff to support the acquisition and allocation of program resources
2. Provides required program resources	Documents showing resources needed at the project or non-project work level and how these resources were acquired
3. Supports organizational strategic planning and budgeting processes	Example: Documents showing changes required to execute the program management plan
4. Uses the program management information system (PMIS) in all phases of program and component management	Example: Use of the PMIS to assist in early identification of resource issues as well as on-going resource allocation activity

ELEMENT 4.3 CHANGE REQUESTS ARE REVIEWED	
PERFORMANCE CRITERIA	TYPES OF EVIDENCE
1. Uses the change control process	Example: The change control system
2. Analyzes change requests from the program's projects or non-project work	Documents showing the impact on the overall program and other projects and non-project work in the program
3. Approves, disapproves, or defers change requests (Program Manager)	Documents showing approval/disapproval/deferral of changes within the program manager's authority
4. Approves, disapproves, or defers change requests (Program Governance Board)	Documents showing approval/disapproval/deferral of changes within the Program Governance Board's authority

ELEMENT 4.4 ADDITIONAL WORK IS AUTHORIZED AS REQUIRED	
PERFORMANCE CRITERIA	TYPES OF EVIDENCE
1. Changes overall projects and non-project work as required	Documents showing— • the business case for a new project or non-project work • updates to the program management plan • the link for a new project to the organization's strategic plan Examples include: Charters for new projects A change in overall priorities based on changes in the program's projects and non-project work

2. Defines the decision-making structure for changes to the program or its projects or non-project work	Documents showing— • the criteria to initiate a new project • the escalation criteria to follow • go/no-go decisions

ELEMENT 4.5 COMMUNICATION WITH STAKEHOLDERS IS FOSTERED AND ENCOURAGED AT ALL LEVELS	
PERFORMANCE CRITERIA	TYPES OF EVIDENCE
1. Collaborates with stakeholders to ensure involvement	Documents showing interaction with stakeholders on the program Examples include: The stakeholder register The stakeholder inventory
2. Communicates with stakeholders throughout the program	Documents showing the strategic objectives and program status provided to stakeholders
3. Follows the program stakeholder management plan	Examples include: Metrics to measure stakeholder engagement activities Tools and techniques used to engage stakeholders Documents showing— • updates to metrics in the stakeholder management plan • any updates to the stakeholder management strategy
4. Prioritizes the impact of stakeholders	Examples include: The stakeholder register A stakeholder tracking and prioritization system Documents showing the urgency and probability of stakeholder-related risks
5. Provides required information to stakeholders	Documents showing ad hoc requests for information Examples include: Stakeholder reports on program status information The communication log
6. Uses a variety of information systems and distribution methods	Examples include: Information gathering and retrieval systems Information distribution methods

ELEMENT 4.6 COMMUNICATION WITH MEMBERS OF THE PROGRAM GOVERNANCE BOARD OCCURS ON A REGULAR BASIS	
PERFORMANCE CRITERIA	TYPES OF EVIDENCE
1. Presents information to the Program Governance Board regularly	Example: Presentations to Program Governance Board members at scheduled and ad hoc meetings Documents showing requests for ad hoc information Example: Program cash flow analysis

| 2. Controls contractual agreements | Documents showing—
• updates to contracts
• contractor performance and status reports
Example: List of contract modifications in the past six months |
| 3. Ensures sponsors are assigned for new projects and non-project work | Example: Documents showing official sponsor identification |

ELEMENT 4.7 ALIGNMENT OF THE PROGRAM'S GOALS, AND ITS BENEFITS, IS ASSESSED AGAINST THAT OF THE ORGANIZATION

PERFORMANCE CRITERIA	TYPES OF EVIDENCE
1. Translates strategic goals into tactical activities	Example: Documents showing the links from each project or non-project work in the program to the strategic goals of the organization
2. Provides suggestions for updates in corporate policies, procedures, and processes	Documents showing— • suggestions and recommendations • audit findings • team suggestions based on lessons learned from the program

ELEMENT 4.8 COMMON ACTIVITIES AMONG THE PROGRAM'S PROJECTS AND NON-PROJECT WORK ARE COORDINATED

PERFORMANCE CRITERIA	TYPES OF EVIDENCE
1. Manages interrelationships among projects and non-project work	Documents showing— • the interrelationships for scope adherence • requested change requests due to interface and integration issues • updates to the program management plan Example: The lessons learned database
2. Follows the communications management plan and stakeholder guidelines	Documents showing updates to the communication plan for modifications requiring additional deliverables

ELEMENT 4.9 DEPENDENCIES WITH OTHER ORGANIZATIONAL INITIATIVES ARE COORDINATED

PERFORMANCE CRITERIA	TYPES OF EVIDENCE
1. Maintains a lessons learned database	Examples include: Updates to the current lessons learned database The organization's knowledge management system
2. Conducts lessons learned sessions with program team members	Documented minutes of lessons learned meetings and any updates to pertinent database

ELEMENT 4.10 THE PROGRAM MANAGEMENT PLAN IS EXECUTED	
PERFORMANCE CRITERIA	TYPES OF EVIDENCE
1. Delivers the intended benefits of the program	Documents showing— • the benefits that have been realized as planned • the deliverables and other work that has been completed • the overall product and service improvements
2. Conducts lessons learned sessions with stakeholders	Documents showing meetings held, including those if the program did not deliver its intended results

5.0 Monitoring and Controlling the Program	
EVALUATING PROGRAM PROGRESS FOR SUCCESSFUL EXECUTION AND BENEFIT REALIZATION	

ELEMENT 5.1 PROGRESS IS ANALYZED ACCORDING TO THE PROGRAM MANAGEMENT PLAN

PERFORMANCE CRITERIA	TYPES OF EVIDENCE
1. Sets up a process to ensure each project in the program or non-project work meets its requirements	Documents showing the process that is used
2. Analyzes progress of projects in the program according to the program management plan as well as the individual project management plans	Documents showing how the program management plan is used, updated, and modified as required Example: The various performance analyses and resulting reports that are produced
3. Determines whether requests for corrective or preventive actions are needed	Documents showing change requests and their disposition by the Program Manager or Program Governance Board
4. Determines whether schedule milestones and budget goals are met	Example: Program performance reports to show status and forecasts to predict the likelihood of achieving planned outcomes
5. Monitors progress of suppliers	Documents showing • contract modifications • change requests to update the procurement management plan Examples include: Supplier performance reports The results of inspections and audits The results of supplier reviews

ELEMENT 5.2 BENEFITS REALIZATION IS ANALYZED ACCORDING TO THE BENEFITS REALIZATION PLAN

PERFORMANCE CRITERIA	TYPES OF EVIDENCE
1. Provides reports and benefits metrics to assess overall program progress in benefits delivery	Examples include: The benefits realization report to show benefits realized versus those in the plan The number of change requests to the benefits realization plan, especially regarding timeliness of the realized benefits The results of stakeholder surveys to see if there is successful benefits delivery
2. Performs benefits realization analysis	Example: The results of the benefits review process to determine the extent to which benefits were delivered, value offered, resources consumed and risks encountered in doing so

| 3. Conducts benefits reviews separately or during a comprehensive program review | Example: Minutes and action items based on the reviews with an emphasis on the value to be provided by each benefit |
| 4. Arranges for or conducts periodic program health checks | Example: Whether the life-cycle costs will exceed the benefits to be realized or whether the benefits will not be delivered on time |

ELEMENT 5.3 ISSUES AND RISKS ARE CONTINUOUSLY IDENTIFIED, AND CORRECTIVE ACTIONS ARE TAKEN AS REQUIRED

PERFORMANCE CRITERIA	TYPES OF EVIDENCE
1. Identifies program-level and component-level risks throughout the life cycle	Documents showing— <ul><li>actions taken to resolve each major risk</li><li>actions used to continually identify risks</li><li>the results of assumptions analysis</li></ul>Example: The program risk register
2. Determines effectiveness of risk responses	Documents showing— <ul><li>the actual response used and analyses of the usefulness of the response</li><li>whether any subsidiary or residual risks resulted from the response</li><li>the use of contingency plans and reserves</li></ul>Example: The trigger conditions
3. Provides oversight of risks at the program level	Documents showing— <ul><li>the results of risk reviews and audits</li><li>the results of program risk review meetings</li><li>the results of lessons learned reviews</li></ul>
4. Identifies, tracks, and resolves program issues	Documents showing— <ul><li>the results of issue management to ensure stakeholder expectations remain aligned with the program's activities and deliverables</li><li>those issues escalated to the Program Governance Board for resolution</li></ul>Example: The tracking system that is used, such as an issue log or register Documents showing— <ul><li>the frequency of updates to the log or register</li><li>updates to the program risk management plan</li></ul>
5. Establishes an issue analysis process	Example: Methods used to assess issue impact and severity Documents showing change requests based on the analysis Example: An issue log

ELEMENT 5.4 *EXTERNAL ENVIRONMENTAL CHANGES ARE ANALYZED TO DETERMINE THE POSSIBLE IMPACT ON THE PROGRAM AND ITS REALIZATION OF BENEFITS*	
PERFORMANCE CRITERIA	TYPES OF EVIDENCE
1. Identifies any external changes that may affect the program and its anticipated benefits	Documents showing— • analysis of these changes and the overall effect on the program and its deliverables and benefits realization • the integration of these external changes with other program changes Example: Results of natural disasters, war, social unrest, competitive environment, political issues, labor problems, materials shortages, inflation, etc.
2. Monitors the program environment	Documents showing changes that could affect overall program direction Example: Program risk register
3. Monitors legal issues	Documents showing legal issues such as insurance programs with class action lawsuits that can change program priorities and scope

ELEMENT 5.5 *GOVERNANCE OVERSIGHT IS REGULARLY PRACTICED AT THE PROGRAM AND PROJECT LEVELS*	
PERFORMANCE CRITERIA	TYPES OF EVIDENCE
1. Communicates regularly with the Program Governance Board	Documents showing interactions to ensure the Program Governance Board has current information on benefits delivery and other pertinent and relevant information on overall program performance Example: A log of the type and frequency of communications
2. Takes corrective and preventive action based on Program Governance Board feedback	Documents showing— • actions taken based on feedback from the Program Governance Board during stage gate meetings, program health checks, or other reviews of program status and compliance • compliance with regulatory and legislative requirements as applicable
3. Provides oversight of program procurements	Example: Strategies, tools, methods, and metrics used

4. Follows the established governance oversight process	Documents showing— • the governance oversight process in use • go/no-go decisions from stage gate reviews Example: A governance decision register Documents showing change requests to update the governance plan
5. Submits closure recommendations	Documents showing closure recommendations for a component project or the program

ELEMENT 5.6 PROGRAM CHANGES ARE IMPLEMENTED IN ACCORDANCE WITH ESTABLISHED INTEGRATED CHANGE CONTROL PROCEDURES	
PERFORMANCE CRITERIA	TYPES OF EVIDENCE
1. Ensures approved changed requests are implemented	Documents showing the program's integrated change control system Example: Change request log with implementation date
2. Assesses impact of approved change requests with other program and project documentation	Documents showing— • the impact on program performance • the impact on program procurements Examples include: Updated program management plan Updated project management plan Updated program scope statement Updated program schedule
3. Informs stakeholders when change requests are approved and implemented	Examples include: Stakeholder register Stakeholder management strategy Communications strategy Stakeholder communications log

ELEMENT 5.7 PROGRAM EXECUTION IS MONITORED ACCORDING TO THE PROGRAM MANAGEMENT PLAN	
PERFORMANCE CRITERIA	TYPES OF EVIDENCE
1. Checks alignment with the plans at the overall program level and at the individual project level	Documents showing— • changes to plans and why they were required • updates to the program management plan based on approved changes
2. Uses a variety of approaches to assess program performance	Documents showing approaches used and their effectiveness in monitoring and controlling program performance
3. Uses the program management information system	Examples include: The system used and metrics collected, monitored, and controlled Program performance reports
4. Assists executives and members of the Program Governance Board to predict the likelihood of achieving planned outcomes	Example: Forecasts based on earned value and use of experts as needed

ELEMENT 5.8 SCHEDULE SLIPPAGES AND OPPORTUNITIES ARE IDENTIFIED AND MANAGED	
PERFORMANCE CRITERIA	TYPES OF EVIDENCE
1. Follows the program's schedule to the greatest extent practicable to produce required deliverables on time	Documents showing— • actual start and finish dates with the planned timeline • updates to the program's master schedule or to individual project schedules • opportunities and slippages • any corrective actions required, including changes to the schedule baseline • opportunities to accelerate the program
2. Analyzes the work of suppliers for schedule impact	Example: Status reports from suppliers Documents showing program payment schedule updates
3. Identifies metrics for schedule monitoring and control	Examples include: The metrics collected The number of activities added to program master schedule every two weeks
ELEMENT 5.9 PROACTIVE COST CONTROL IS PRACTICED	
PERFORMANCE CRITERIA	TYPES OF EVIDENCE
1. Analyzes actual versus planned costs on a regular basis	Documents showing— • progress according to the financial management plan • the impact to the program's projects from overruns or under-runs • actual program expenditures to ensure costs are within established parameters Examples: Profit and loss reports, cash flow reports, and/or accounts receivables and accounts payables
2. Identifies opportunities to return funding to the enterprise	Example: Documents showing expenditures to see if the allocated budget is required
3. Conducts trend analyses to predict problems	Documents showing possible financial problems and how they were handled Example: The use of earned value analysis to monitor progress Documents showing revised forecasts and estimates at completion
4. Analyzes work of suppliers for cost impact	Documents showing the results of contract performance reviews Example: The use of a budget management system Documents showing— • updates to the program budget baseline • updates to the program budget • payments to contractors

5. Establishes a cost management system	Examples include: A system to show impacts of overruns and under-runs A system to show costs involving the program infrastructure
6. Conducts financial status reviews	Documents showing— • action items and corrective action taken based on reviews concerning compliance with contracts and the cost baseline • updates to the cost baseline if changes are approved • closure of project budgets

ELEMENT 5.10 STAKEHOLDER EXPECTATIONS ARE MANAGED	
PERFORMANCE CRITERIA	TYPES OF EVIDENCE
1. Communicates with stakeholders to resolve issues and concerns	Documents showing the frequency of stakeholder interaction Example: A stakeholder communications log
2. Uses a variety of negotiation techniques in working with stakeholders with conflicting interests	Documents showing decisions reached when stakeholders have conflicting requirements
3. Monitors stakeholder participation	Documents showing— • stakeholder participation in meeting minutes, reports, etc. • updates to the stakeholder management strategy • updates to the stakeholder management plan • updates to the communications management plan
4. Keeps stakeholders apprised of program status regularly	Examples include: Reports provided to different categories of stakeholders Metrics collected to show the extent of stakeholder involvement by group or category
5. Uses conflict resolution techniques to manage conflicts between stakeholders	Documents showing outcomes of conflicts between stakeholders and their resolution Example: The number of conflicts requiring resolution to the Program Governance Board

ELEMENT 5.11 PERFORMANCE DATA ARE CONSOLIDATED TO DETERMINE APPROPRIATE RESOURCE USE TO DELIVER BENEFITS	
PERFORMANCE CRITERIA	TYPES OF EVIDENCE
1. Consolidates program status data from the individual projects and non-project work of the program	Example: Status reports that are prepared Documents showing methods used to gather and compile status information
2. Employs the program reporting process to obtain regular status information from program procurements	Examples include: Procurement status reports Program reports The communication management plan
3. Provides resource allocation and use reports to stakeholder to show how benefits will be delivered	Examples include: Performance reports Program presentations Resource histograms Documents showing feedback from stakeholders
4. Uses the established Information Distribution process to provide reports to stakeholders	Example: The Information Distribution process used
5. Establishes time and cost reporting systems	Documents showing the systems and how they are used Example: The use of earned value analysis
6. Conducts regular program-level status review meetings	Example: Meeting minutes and action items Documents showing the meetings and the stakeholders involved
ELEMENT 5.12 COMPONENTS TRANSITION TO CLOSURE	
PERFORMANCE CRITERIA	TYPES OF EVIDENCE
1. Determines when a project or other component is ready for closure	Documents showing closure recommendations by the program manager or the Program Governance Board

6.0 Closing the Program	
FORMALIZING PROGRAM ACCEPTANCE AND COMPLETION	
ELEMENT 6.1 THE PROGRAM IS FORMALLY CLOSED	
PERFORMANCE CRITERIA	TYPES OF EVIDENCE
1. Obtains final acceptance from the sponsor and customer(s)	Documents showing— • all program work is complete • acceptance of products, services, and results from the sponsor or customer Example: The program's archives Documents showing that the Program Governance Board accepts program closure recommendations
2. Releases all program resources	Example: A template from a resource management plan showing that resources are released according to schedule, both physical (materials, facilities, etc.) and human
3. Provides performance feedback to team members	Evidence that the program manager met with the team member to provide one-on-one feedback Evidence that the program manager met with the functional manager to discuss team member performance Documents showing that improvements in team member performance and attendance at training courses are provided to the human resources department or appropriate group
4. Closes program financial activities	Documents showing— • feedback from the financial department that the program is completed • whether warnings were provided of any potential for the program to exceed its budget • whether any infractions occurred and, if so, how they were resolved • whether updates were needed to the budget baseline • all project budgets and the program budget are closed Example: A full-scope verification audit and accounting of financial records
5. Closes the program management plan	Documents showing— • all requirements in each of the subsidiary program plans have been met • all active projects have been closed

ELEMENT 6.2 PRODUCTS AND SERVICES TRANSITION TO OPERATIONS	
PERFORMANCE CRITERIA	TYPES OF EVIDENCE
1. Transitions the product or service and all operational work to the client (internal or external)	Documents showing— • acceptance by operations is obtained • the requirements in the program transition plan have been satisfied
2. Reallocates program resources to other activities in the organization	Documents showing— • the program resource plan was followed and that resources were reallocated as planned • assurance resources will be available to work on closeout activities before they are released to other areas or other programs and projects • assurance that critical team members will be available if needed after they are released to answer questions and support the transition

ELEMENT 6.3 PROGRAM BENEFITS ARE REALIZED	
PERFORMANCE CRITERIA	TYPES OF EVIDENCE
1. Evaluates the actual benefits realized	Documents showing the extent to which stated benefits were realized Example: The benefits realization report Documents showing that items in the program's charter have been met
2. Surveys program stakeholders to assess their level of satisfaction with program results	Example: Feedback from stakeholders Documents showing meetings with stakeholders as needed to discuss outstanding issues

ELEMENT 6.4 CUSTOMER SUPPORT IS PROVIDED (AS APPLICABLE, SUCH AS DEFINED IN A CONTRACT)	
PERFORMANCE CRITERIA	TYPES OF EVIDENCE
1. Provides support to customers as necessary	Documents showing— • the program has met the requirements of its business case • the goals of the program versus those achieved • assurance that team members will be accessible if necessary to answer customer questions Example: A customer support plan
2. Provides support if specified by the contract	Documents showing that any support detailed in a contract is followed in terms of guidance and maintenance

ELEMENT 6.5 LESSONS LEARNED ARE INTEGRATED INTO THE ORGANIZATION'S KNOWLEDGE MANAGEMENT SYSTEM	
PERFORMANCE CRITERIA	TYPES OF EVIDENCE
1. Publishes lessons learned	Example: Availability of lessons learned in an accessible format Documents reviews and updates program documents Example: Incorporating lessons learned into the program's final report Documents showing— • a list of outcomes of actions in risk management • meeting with the team on lessons learned before a transition to the knowledge management system
ELEMENT 6.6 FEEDBACK IS PROVIDED ON AREAS OUTSIDE THE SCOPE OF THE PROGRAM	
PERFORMANCE CRITERIA	TYPES OF EVIDENCE
1. Analyzes program results for impacts that can affect other areas of the organization	Documents showing other lessons learned outside the scope of the program but which may benefit other parts of the organization
2. Surveys the team and key stakeholders for areas of improvement in the program management practice	Documents giving suggestions to improve the overall practice of program management based on lessons learned from this program
ELEMENT 6.7 PROGRAM DOCUMENTS ARE ARCHIVED FOR FUTURE REUSE	
PERFORMANCE CRITERIA	TYPES OF EVIDENCE
1. Updates organizational processes, procedures, policies, and guidelines (organizational process assets)	Documents showing— • any changes to the organizational process assets during the course of the program • the technical and programmatic history of baselines
2. Prepares a final program report	Documents critical information that can assist future programs Example: The final program report

3. Follows the program's documentation archive plan	Documents showing that requirements in the program's archive plan have been met Example: Archives and indexes of program documents for future reuse or for any future audits

ELEMENT 6.8 CONTRACTUAL OBLIGATIONS ARE MET	
PERFORMANCE CRITERIA	TYPES OF EVIDENCE
1. Meets all contractual requirements (the perspective here is that the program manager is in the seller's organization)	Documents showing— • all deliverables required in the contract(s) have been delivered and accepted by the performing organization • payments have been made in a timely fashion Example: Information provided to stakeholders when contracts are officially closed
2. Performs supplier performance reviews (the perspective here is that the program manager's organization has hired contractors to assist in the programmatic effort)	Documents showing— • results of reviews to note strengths and weaknesses of suppliers and whether they should be added to or retained on the qualified supplier list • the extent of any delays or disruptions to the program's schedule or objectives based on not achieving any planned commitments • any corrective actions to suppliers • whether legal remedies in the suppliers' contract's terms and conditions were implemented Example: The number and nature of the change requests issued to suppliers
3. Reconciles budget allocation	Documents showing— • the financial analysis undertaken to compare actual contract costs to contract budget • that any remaining budget allocations are returned to the overall program budget

4. Conducts procurement audits and a contract closeout audit	Documents showing— • whether the contractual deliverables were met according to the Statement of Work and other contract terms and conditions • warranties were met (as applicable) Example: Procurement documents to determine if contract closure requirements were met Documents showing changes made based on recommendations from the procurement audits Example: The contract closeout audit report
5. Prepares a procurement performance report	Documents showing— • the results of supplier reviews that are distributed to stakeholders • lessons learned during the procurement process • whether changes are required to the contract closure procedure

ELEMENT 6.9 INTELLECTUAL PROPERTY IS CAPTURED FOR REUSE	
PERFORMANCE CRITERIA	TYPES OF EVIDENCE
1. Releases resources after ensuring that intellectual property obtained during the program is retained	Documents showing— • proof that intellectual property is retained • any confidentiality agreements are followed

ELEMENT 6.10 A LEGACY OF BENEFIT SUSTAINMENT IS ACHIEVED	
PERFORMANCE CRITERIA	TYPES OF EVIDENCE
1. Providing ongoing support for the new product or service delivered by the program	Documents showing support for the new product or service Example: Customer support process and operations, including maintenance records, repair logs, and customer comment file
2. Using resources to maintain and ensure customer satisfaction	Documents showing— • resources are available to assist the customer • the customer's use of the new product or service in terms of the customer's expectations
3. Providing support to manage post-production updates	Examples include: Providing project management services as needed through a new project to focus on delivering upgrades to the product Methods to optimize the value of the new product or service to provide additional benefits

Personal Competencies

While the preceding section discussed performance competencies, a program manager's personal competencies are equally important in the successful delivery of the program's benefits and deliverables. This section describes the eight personal competencies required by most program managers most of the time.

1.0 Unit of Competence: Communicating	
USES A VARIETY OF APPROACHES TO EFFECTIVELY COMMUNICATE WITH STAKEHOLDERS	
ELEMENT 1.1 ACTIVELY LISTENS, UNDERSTANDS, AND RESPONDS TO STAKEHOLDERS	
PERFORMANCE CRITERIA	TYPES OF EVIDENCE
1. Actively listens	Examples include: Paying close attention to the speaker Requesting the speaker to repeat information if it is not clearly understood Using words that do not have double meanings associated with them Showing empathy for the points of view of others Documents showing responses to issues raised by others and action items that are taken
2. Encourages effective communication in self and others	Documents showing problems associated with stakeholder's lack of receipt of key information Examples include: Being "present" and attentive during each communication Making sure communications are reciprocal and not one way Active involvement of the program management team and other stakeholders in communications
3. Acknowledges receipt of both implicit and explicit communications	Documents showing observations from communications Example: Being aware of both the content of the communications and the methods used to convey them
4. Responds to and acts on stakeholder expectations, concerns, and issues	Documents showing— • the best ways to communicate with the various stakeholder groups • messages have been received and when a response will be provided

	• a way to track each message until it is resolved Example: Meets with small groups of stakeholders, to determine the best approach to address their concerns
5. Actively addresses the issues and obstacles associated with communications on global programs	Demonstrates an understanding of time zone issues by scheduling meetings so that one group is not always inconvenienced Documents key cultural considerations in global communications Demonstrates sensitivity to language differences Examples include: Sends messages in writing first to enable team members to read and understand the message before speaking on the matter Appreciates individual differences in communications styles through patience and understanding

ELEMENT 1.2 USES THE KEY CHANNELS OF COMMUNICATIONS	
PERFORMANCE CRITERIA	TYPES OF EVIDENCE
1. Engages stakeholders regularly and proactively	Documents showing— • stakeholder communications requirements have been met • communication flow (e.g., who will communicate with whom) Examples include: Recognition of the three key receiving parties/communications channels—customers, sponsors, and component managers—but not forgetting other stakeholders Informal communications to continually reach out to stakeholders
2. Quickly and effectively distributes information	Example: The use of the program's information distribution process Documents showing— • the effectiveness of the communication by using informal conversations, surveys, presentations, and observations • confirmation that the information was received and when it was received Example: Using change requests as needed and providing notification of responses to these requests to stakeholders

3. Emphasizes both formal and informal communications	Documents showing— • the type of communication method used • various informal methods for day-to-day activities and formal methods for overall status on a periodic and regularly scheduled basis Example: Minutes from meetings, brainstorming sessions, use of the Delphi technique, and SWOT analyses Documents showing— • follow-up activities • feedback of availability to meet with stakeholders as needed for follow-up and clarification

ELEMENT 1.3 ENSURES THE QUALITY OF THE INFORMATION THAT IS COMMUNICATED

PERFORMANCE CRITERIA	TYPES OF EVIDENCE
1. Uses different information sources	Documents showing— • information sources used • feedback received from these sources
2. Provides information that is accurate, complete, and factual	Documents showing the analysis conducted of the value of the information provided Example: Presentations given to different audiences and written progress reports
3. Provides consistent messages to stakeholders	Documents showing that factual information is provided Example: The use of different communication messages, such as e-mails, reports, voice mails, and presentations Demonstrates that the message is clearly considered before it is provided to the stakeholders by reviewing with others
4. Seeks validation of information	Example: The use of expert judgment, especially from subject matter experts, interest groups, and professional associations

ELEMENT 1.4 TAILORS THE INFORMATION TO THE AUDIENCE

PERFORMANCE CRITERIA	TYPES OF EVIDENCE
1. Provides necessary and relevant information in a form each audience can understand	Documents showing feedback from stakeholders that they have received and understood the information provided Example: Presentation skills
2. Determines the most suitable approach for the audience	Example: Using a stakeholder analysis to determine the preferred communications approach Documents showing the approach in the stakeholder management strategy

	Documents showing information from stakeholders to verify the usefulness of the approach selected
3. Presents the communication in a way that maximizes its understanding and acceptance	Demonstrates sensitivity to each stakeholder by choosing the time, method, and place to communicate critical information Example: The ability to use different approaches to communicate Documents minutes and action items from team meetings, stakeholder meetings, and presentations Example: The location selected, time selected, people involved, and any privacy concerns

ELEMENT 1.5 EFFECTIVELY USES EACH OF THE DIFFERENT COMMUNICATIONS DIMENSIONS*

PERFORMANCE CRITERIA	TYPES OF EVIDENCE
1. Employs the most appropriate approach for each circumstance	Example: Internal and external, formal and informal, oral and written, official and unofficial, and verbal and nonverbal
2. Uses different communications skills based on the dimension and audience	Example: The use of "I" messages (showing that one is taking responsibility for one's actions) and open-ended questions (to avoid yes-or-no type answers)
3. Recognizes and overcomes communications barriers	Example: Projection (or assuming others have one's same concerns), displacement (passing on a strong belief that one has in one setting to another when it is not appropriate to do so), and objectification (putting people into categories, which may or may not be appropriate)

* Communication Dimensions referred to are internal and external; formal and informal; oral and written; official and unofficial; and verbal and nonverb.

2.0 Unit of Competence: Leading

USES A VARIETY OF APPROACHES TO LEAD THE PROGRAM AND ENSURE THERE IS A SHARED VISION AS TO ITS IMPORTANCE

ELEMENT 2.1 IMPLEMENTS THE PROGRAM'S VISION

PERFORMANCE CRITERIA	TYPES OF EVIDENCE
1. Actively engages with stakeholders to strategically sell the program's vision	Examples include: A kick-off meeting with the program team Individual meetings with key stakeholders, both internal and external Using an interactive approach in discussing the vision for mutual understanding and commitment Documents showing stakeholder feedback to ensure a common understanding of the program's vision
2. Continually discusses the vision at meetings to reinforce the message throughout the program life cycle	Examples include: Discussions of the vision at each team meeting; meetings of the Program Governance Board; meetings with the portfolio review board or a similar group that convenes to approve new programs for consideration or to determine priorities among programs in progress; and, meetings with key stakeholders Presentations given that note the vision in explaining the program Documents showing feedback received
3. Reviews documents prepared by project managers to see if the vision is Incorporated in each program component	Examples include: Project charters and project management plans Participating in kick-off meetings of new projects in the program where the vision is reinforced Documents showing presentations given by project managers
4. Reviews the business case for new projects for alignment with the program's vision	Documents showing— • any differences as noted in the business case and the stated vision for the program • the feedback provided to offer suggestions before the business case is presented to the Program Governance Board and/or portfolio review board

5. Recognizes if changes in the external environment lead to the need to change the program's vision	Examples include: Monitoring trends in the environment or in the organization's overall strategic plan Presentations of the need for a programmatic change of direction to the Program Governance Board Documents showing— • a required change through the change request process if applicable • stakeholders have been informed of any changes

ELEMENT 2.2 ESTABLISHES THE PROGRAM'S DIRECTION	
PERFORMANCE CRITERIA	TYPES OF EVIDENCE
1. Identifies and communicates critical success factors to all stakeholders	Example: Use of the benefits realization plan Documents showing survey results with key stakeholders concerning the success of the program Examples include: Use of focus groups and the Delphi approach to identify critical success factors Asking probing questions to clarify perceptions of the program Documents showing meetings with each customer and key stakeholder group to gain understanding of what is meant by success
2. Actively negotiates for needed program resources	Examples include: Use of knowledge, skills, and competency profiles Use of the resource plan to pinpoint where critical skills are lacking The ability to persuade people to join the program because of its importance to the organization Use knowledge of the organization and its "power brokers" to get the best people on the program team
3. Discusses program goals with the team to make sure they are clear	Examples include: One-on-one and group meetings to discuss program goals and ways to accomplish them Ensuring that all suppliers and vendors understand their part in achieving individual or multiple program goals Discussing with functional managers and other stakeholders who have responsibility for project or task completion concerning the importance of their work in achieving goals Documents showing program goals through meeting minutes and the program charter

4. Prepares a program roadmap	Example: Presentations of the roadmap to stakeholders, the team, and the governance board Documents showing— • any feedback obtained before finalizing the roadmap • buy-in through sign-off on the roadmap by key stakeholders • a bridge between the program activities and expected benefits Example: Communications with stakeholders about the high-level scope and execution approach for the program

ELEMENT 2.3 RECOGNIZES THE INTERDEPENDENCIES WITHIN THE PROGRAM

PERFORMANCE CRITERIA	TYPES OF EVIDENCE
1. Performs component analysis	Documents showing how each component interfaces with other components in the program Example: Presentations of the results of the component analysis to the team, the Program Governance Board, and other key stakeholders Documents showing the performance of each component to ensure it remains aligned with the program's overall strategy
2. Reviews existing projects and other work for inclusion into the program	Documents showing— • the interdependencies between projects in the program, especially given resource constraints • the results of feasibility studies • the results of comparative advantage analyses Example: Presentations of the results of reviews and obtaining feedback
3. Assimilates existing projects and non-project work into the program as directed	Examples include: Meeting with stakeholders on existing projects and non-project work to discuss why they will be part of the program Working with project managers to ensure project documentation is updated to show it is now part of the program Presentations on the importance of inclusion of these projects in the program because of specific interdependencies Documents showing feedback from presentations

4. Recommends that new projects are part of the program	Documents showing interdependencies between new projects and the existing projects in the program Examples include: The business case for the new project Presentations of the importance of the new project to the Program Governance Board and to the portfolio review board Meetings with other key stakeholders to discuss the proposed new project, its interdependencies with others in the program, and its benefits Documents showing feedback from these meetings
5. Recommends existing projects to be terminated	Documents showing— • status reports and presentations • benefits achieved versus those expected • completed deliverables • any continued interdependencies with other projects in the program • a termination request to the Program Governance Board to either close the project or to terminate it Examples include: Presentation of the decision to the Program Governance Board Meetings with key stakeholders to discuss the decision Assisting the project manager in transitioning benefits if the project is complete Assisting the project manager in redistributing resources Documents showing— • all closure activities of the project are complete • results of surveys of the team for improvements to the program processes • results of surveys of the customers for improvement suggestions Example: Using changes requests to implement improvement ideas if appropriate Documents showing implementation and updates to other artifacts

ELEMENT 2.4 TAKES CALCULATED RISKS; IS VENTURESOME	
PERFORMANCE CRITERIA	TYPES OF EVIDENCE
1. Takes risks on new ideas if they look promising	Examples include: Conducting a risk vs. opportunity analysis meeting with program team members Using numerous risk analysis techniques such as decision trees, pair-wise comparison, Delphi method, and the nominal group technique to help make risk-based decisions Including suppliers, vendors, and parties outside the program to help think through ideas Makes a decision to move forward in the face of uncertainty following the 70% principle (having only 70% of the available information) Documents showing the decision in program file
2. Demonstrates the "nerve" to move ahead when others might be more cautious	Examples include: Working with project managers and the program team to implement new ideas to maximize the opportunity in the face of uncertainty Showing confidence in the decision, not back-tracking or engaging in "hand wringing" for having made the decision Building confidence in others that the direction chosen is the right one Documents showing the approach used for future lessons learned analysis
3. Is willing to try a new, good idea despite the objections of others	Examples include: Moving forward with a decision despite the intransigence of others Working with those opposed to the new idea to have them assist in its implementation and success Documents showing— • the results of the idea being implemented • the results of the corrective actions selected for lessons learned
4. Forecasts the future in an attempt to keep ahead of the changing program environment	Examples include: Constantly reading and reaching out to others to detect opportunities for improvement or enhancement to the program's product or service Doing market research and analysis to determine extent to which competitors will launch similar products or services

	Analyzing the program's stakeholder environment to detect changes in attitudes, perceptions, or personnel, that could either hurt or help the program Analyzing program team members to detect changes in attitudes in perceptions to ensure key members are satisfied and will remain until the program closes Analyzing the broader program supplier environment to detect such issues as work stoppages, labor shortages, dramatic commodity price increases (or decreases), inflation, taxation, and other external risks that could help or hurt the program

ELEMENT 2.5 ASSUMES OWNERSHIP OF THE PROGRAM

PERFORMANCE CRITERIA	TYPES OF EVIDENCE

1. Demonstrates ownership for the program; has a strong sense of accountability	Examples include:
	  Active involvement with members of the Program Governance Board, portfolio review board, and other stakeholders, both internal and external
	  Responding as soon as possible to concerns expressed by stakeholders, delays, or risks by taking preventive or corrective actions
	  Taking ownership for adverse program outcomes
	  Documents showing where the program manager took responsibility for any program problems

2. Aligns personal priorities to the increased probability of program success as measured by delivery of program benefits	Examples include:
	  A documented Individual Development Plan
	  Specific objectives in one's performance plan
	  Documents showing a priority list of action items

3. Supports and promotes actions of the program team and the project managers	Examples include:
	  Surveys of feedback from the team and project managers as to ways the program manager can improve his or her leadership of the program
	  Feedback from the team and project managers that the program manager is acting assertively on their behalf
	  Including project managers in meetings with the Program Governance Board at key stage gate reviews

	Documents showing notes from meetings that show support for the actions of the team and the project managers Examples include: Showing awareness of the project manager's activities through one-on-one meetings, status reports, and occasional attendance at the project manager's team meetings Taking a stand at meetings with the customer, the Program Governance Board, and the portfolio review board to support project managers' actions and team actions as his or her own
4. Monitors and controls the program throughout its life cycle	Examples include: Collecting, measuring, and distributing performance data to stakeholders Assessing trends and taking corrective actions as required Forecasts of future performance to point to areas in need of correction and to predict the likelihood of success Documents showing the results of program performance analyses Example: Using gap analysis in terms of cost, schedule, or anticipated benefits

3.0 Unit of Competence: Building Relationships	
WORKS ACTIVELY TO BUILD RELATIONSHIPS WITH PROGRAM STAKEHOLDERS	
ELEMENT 3.1 BUILDS TRUST AMONG STAKEHOLDERS, CLIENTS, AND TEAM MEMBERS	
PERFORMANCE CRITERIA	TYPES OF EVIDENCE
1. Identifies stakeholders with active involvement as well as those who have only a peripheral interest	Documents showing how the program will affect different types of stakeholders, focusing on those who support the program to ensure trust is established Examples include: Using the strategic plan to identify the scope and types of stakeholders who may be involved Formal and informal communications channels used to interact with stakeholders
2. Demonstrates genuine interest in stakeholder issues, concerns, and opinions	Examples include: Acting on stakeholder concerns by promptly resolving issues Conducting brainstorming sessions with stakeholders to identify solutions to issues Follow-up communications with stakeholders to assess their level of satisfaction with problem resolution Following through on actions identified Documents showing stakeholder communications activities
3. Confides in stakeholders by volunteering information and providing important details about program activities	Examples include: Openly, but judiciously, discussing programmatic and team issues to help resolve problems Promoting a "win-win" attitude between and among stakeholder groups; is always seen as promoting the program's goals over individual ones Continuously reaching out to stakeholders to discuss the program's vision, progress, and issues Maintaining an "open-door" policy Delivering consistent messages to various stakeholders regarding program matters

ELEMENT 3.2 LEVERAGES THE ORGANIZATION'S POLITICAL DYNAMICS TO PROMOTE PROGRAM GOALS	
PERFORMANCE CRITERIA	TYPES OF EVIDENCE
1. Garners support with the right people for his or her ideas for program direction and change	Examples include: Formal and informal meetings with key stakeholders to discuss program direction, issues, and concerns Ad hoc, one-on-one meetings with specific individuals to discuss key issues Seeking advice from key constituents regarding program management matters
2. Understands the organization's internal dynamics and approaches work accordingly	Examples include: Reviewing organizational charts noting key interfaces with the Enterprise Program Management Office Asking more tenured professionals and executives not associated with the program where the organization's power base is located Asking more tenured professionals to introduce him or her to key executives and others who may provide critical assistance in various aspects of program execution Reviewing and understanding key organizational policies, procedures, and processes that govern actions of the team members in program execution
3. Keeps in touch with multiple sources to better interpret internal politics	Examples include: Establishing a network of trusted sources who will keep him or her apprised of internal developments, personnel matters, power base shifts, and other information that could impact the program Reading internal newsletters, press releases, annual reports, memoranda, and other documentation that provide newsworthy information about the organization and its key players Establishing "alerts" on various search engines to keep apprised of organizational developments Meeting with suppliers and vendors who work in various parts of the organization to better understand issues that may not arise using formal reporting mechanisms

4. Anticipates key stakeholders' reaction to change and other events	Examples include: "Testing" ideas with various stakeholders before they are implemented to gauge possible reaction Establishing an informal "steering committee" or "board of directors" of influential stakeholders to discuss key issues and concerns in advance of more formal reporting mechanisms Consulting the organization's legal staff in advance of any possible legal action to gauge any impact on the program Always being forthright and honest when questioned by stakeholders on any program issue

ELEMENT 3.3 ADVOCATES FOR DIVERSITY AND TREATS OTHERS WITH COURTESY AND RESPECT

PERFORMANCE CRITERIA	TYPES OF EVIDENCE
1. Builds a team whose members are diverse in terms of race, ethnic origin, gender, religion, sexual orientation, professional experience, etc. to the greatest extent practicable	Examples include: A program management team consisting of individuals with varied backgrounds and points of view Articulating a vision for diversity in the program, including how the program will benefit being more inclusive Establishing as broad an umbrella for diversity that makes sense for the program and the organization in which it is housed The demonstrated support of top management by including key executives in discussions of why diversity is important in the workplace Staying in touch with program team members through meetings with individuals, group meetings, or focus groups to assess their view of team dynamics Communicating the rationale for promotions to ensure people understand the achievements of the person being promoted To the extent the organization promotes diversity, adheres to organizational policies and practices Documents showing feedback from varied stakeholder groups
2. Treats people with courtesy and respect	Demonstrating courtesy by allowing people to express their points of view freely and openly Abiding by cultural norms so as not to offend various stakeholders Addressing individuals using proper and appropriate titles, etc.

	Using appropriate language in all circumstances Always acting in a professional manner and expecting others to do the same Providing equal treatment to all individuals regardless of rank, race, gender, or other qualifying criteria
3. Uses participative problem-solving to address issues and concerns	Examples include: Encouraging team members to offer ideas even if they are contrary to current thinking Asking functional managers for assistance in problem solving Encouraging all team members to speak out and offer opinions without having to be asked Seeking guidance from team members and others on handling and dealing with new problems

ELEMENT 3.4 ESTABLISHES AND DEMONSTRATES HIGH STANDARDS FOR PERSONAL AND TEAM MEMBER PERFORMANCE

PERFORMANCE CRITERIA	TYPES OF EVIDENCE
1. Establishes realistic program and individual performance goals and standards	Documents showing each team member's individual performance plan for the program that aligns with overall program goals and objectives Example: Team member individual performance criteria Documents showing team members understand what is expected of them in terms of behavior, promptness, Example: Development of or use of an existing Employee Handbook Documents showing the program has adequate quality assurance and control practices designed to deliver the intended result to the client Example: Developing a Quality Assurance and Control Plan Documents showing contractors understand performance goals and deliver products or services in conformance to the contract specifications Example: Inspection reports

2. Monitors and controls all aspects of program and individual performance	Documents showing meetings with team members regularly to review their performance plan and assess progress Example: Performance Improvement Plan for a specific team member Documents showing meetings with the Program Governance Board regularly to review program status and performance Example: Program Status Review Report, noting exceptional performance as well as deficiencies Documents showing continuously tracing contractor deliverables to ensure timeliness and adherence to specifications
3. Continuously seeks to raise standards in self and others	Examples include: Actively taking responsibility for all actions, and avoids blaming others Offering constructive criticism at the appropriate time and place Establishing substantive and meaningful goals for program team members and other stakeholders Establishing broad-based goals for the program team Being reliable and constantly demonstrating a strong work ethic Seeking to improve knowledge on a regular and continuing basis through a variety of means such as training, reading, attending professional society meetings, or discussing issues with peers

ELEMENT 3.5 PROMOTES AND DEMONSTRATES ETHICS, INTEGRITY, AND ADHERENCE TO CORPORATE VALUES IN ALL INTERACTIONS

PERFORMANCE CRITERIA	TYPES OF EVIDENCE
1. Ensures each team member understands his or her ethical responsibility and adherence to corporate values	Examples include: Conducting a meeting in which the corporate ethics standards and values are presented Team members signing ethics or conflict-of-interest statements Issuing each team member a card or document enumerating the corporate values Providing a description of adherence to ethics and values as well as descriptions of noncompliance Distributing copies of the code of conduct (e.g., organizations, professional associations, etc.) to all team members, including business partners if applicable

2. Establishes a process for enforcing the ethics code	Examples include:
	    Documenting the process that addresses consequences for violating it, among other relevant information
	    Implementing the enforcement procedures evenly and objectively across the program
	    Documents showing how the ethics procedures will be applied at the program level

3. Promotes integrity in all interactions	Examples include:
	    Behaving honestly; providing facts, not smokescreens; confronting dishonesty; and challenging any system that encourages dishonesty or rewards
	    Ensuring that ethical behavior is practiced by all on the program by encouraging people to express concerns about questionable practices and reviewing ethical concerns with team members and others
	    Avoiding political and self-serving behavior by focusing on job competence, sharing recognition, and being a team player
	    Courageously standing up for doing the right thing under all circumstances by always having a positive attitude when faced with objections, working to gain cooperation and support from key stakeholders, and encouraging others to speak up and voice their concerns
	    Striving to be a role model for the organization's values by walking the talk, always performing at the highest levels, and actively coaching others to do the same

4.0 Unit of Competence: Negotiating
SEEKS SOLUTIONS TO BUILD WINNING RELATIONSHIPS WITH THOSE INVOLVED ON THE PROGRAM

ELEMENT 4.1 OBTAINS NEEDED PROGRAM RESOURCES	
PERFORMANCE CRITERIA	TYPES OF EVIDENCE
1. Works with the team and other stakeholders in make-or-buy analyses	Documents showing— • the make-or-buy criteria to be used • the results of alternative analyses • feedback received as analyses were performed Examples include: Using objectivity in determining criteria to follow based on sessions with the team and other stakeholders Keeping team members apprised when a decision was to use outsourcing or off-shoring in lieu of in-house resources
2. Works with functional managers to obtain needed resources	Example: Early involvement to explain the importance of the program to functional managers through one-on-one or group settings Documents showing— • preparation of a resource plan with involvement by affected organizations • the specific knowledge, skills, and competencies required for the program • the roles and responsibilities people will be expected to perform on the program • factual information was provided concerning the need for specific resources Examples include: Using strong negotiation skills Using actively listening to show an understanding of the functional managers' points of view Documents showing feedback from stakeholders that the program manager used standards of professionalism in negotiation rather than working for personal gain Example: Demonstrating strong presentation skills
3. Uses experts and third parties as needed to persuade others	Examples include: Using positional power as a way to negotiate for needed resources with functional managers Using a third party to negotiate with functional managers on the importance of the need for specific resources

ELEMENT 4.2 ENSURES PROGRAM ALIGNMENT WITH THE ORGANIZATION'S STRATEGIES	
PERFORMANCE CRITERIA	TYPES OF EVIDENCE
1. Recognizes that organizational priorities change	Documents showing feedback on changes outside the program that affect the organization Example: Communicating with strategic planners and the portfolio manager on effects of the changes to the program Documents showing— • feedback when the organization's strategic goals change • feedback that the program manager used a "can-do" attitude when priorities changed and affected the program Example: Demonstrating a positive attitude while dealing with program challenges
2. Works actively with key executives, strategic planners, and other influencers to ensure program alignment in terms of organizational priorities	Documents showing feedback of the need to adjust the program's vision and deliverables if factors affect the program's overall priority in the organization Example: Presentations concerning the need to change that focus on the revised vision, mission, and values Documents showing feedback regarding awareness of the strategic value of the program Example: Support by the team and other stakeholders to the revised vision Documents showing feedback from the strategic planners that the program manager demonstrated an action-oriented approach Example: Defining new projects and other work, and terminating others to support the organization's revised goals
3. Negotiates competing priorities to make balanced decisions	Examples include: Working with component project managers to determine the priority of human resources, material, and any other needs to determine order of priority Ensuring that program team members, under the guidance of the Program Governance Board or client, assess the priority of cost vs. time vs. scope to help guide decision making Independently making decisions in the absence of policies, procedures, direction, or supervision to drive the program forward Quickly bringing together the key decision makers to discuss key issues to reach a decision and move forward without delay

4. Seeks opportunities to enhance the program's value to the organization	Examples include:
	  Recognizing when a new project could add value to the overall benefits the program could deliver
	  Presentations to describe how to better enhance the program's benefits to the organization
	  Documents showing feedback from the Program Governance Board and other stakeholder groups concerning ideas to enhance value
	Examples include:
	  Using a log to list opportunities
	  Using brainstorming sessions, focus groups, questionnaires and surveys, and other meetings to discuss opportunities to enhance value
	  Documents showing suggestions received
	Examples include:
	  Using a log to show suggestions proposed for implementation through a change request form
	  Showing where support was given even though the program's goals differed from one's personal preferences

5. Consolidates opportunities and presents them to the Program Governance Board and other key stakeholders	Documents showing—
	• meeting notes when opportunities were analyzed
	• use of the integrated change control process
	• proposals to indicate added value to pursue these opportunities
	Examples include:
	  Metrics to show the number of opportunities identified and later pursued
	  Metrics to show how the change added value to the program and the organization

ELEMENT 4.3 WORKS PROACTIVELY WITH THE PROGRAM GOVERNANCE BOARD (BOARD)	
PERFORMANCE CRITERIA	TYPES OF EVIDENCE

1. Views each Board meeting positively	Examples include:
	  Distributing an agenda in advance
	  Distributing minutes taken during the meeting as soon as possible
	  Positive acceptance of feedback and ideas from Board members

2. Seeks ideas of Board members	Examples include: 　Regular surveys of Board members for ideas as 　　to ways to improve program performance 　Using change requests to implement 　　suggestions 　Presentations given 　Documents showing— 　　• suggestions received 　　• meeting notes from one-on-one sessions with 　　　Board members 　Example: Maintaining open lines of 　　communication with Board members
3. Maintains commitments made to 　Board members	Example: Tracking the status of each decision Documents showing the status in implementing 　Board decisions Example: Presentations to update Board 　members of implemented decisions

ELEMENT 4.4 PROMOTES OVERALL STAKEHOLDER SUPPORT

PERFORMANCE CRITERIA	TYPES OF EVIDENCE
1. Applies appropriate negotiating styles 　for each stakeholder or stakeholder 　group	Examples: Using different styles in different 　situations Documents showing— 　• the effectiveness of the use of different styles 　• the use of alternatives analysis Example: The use of facilitating and influencing 　skills Documents showing feedback from stakeholders 　on the result of negotiations
2. Uses experts or third parties to 　promote support	Examples include: 　Using positional power in negotiating with 　　stakeholders or stakeholder groups 　Using a third party, such as a subject matter 　　expert or a neutral party, to assist in 　　negotiations 　Using networking to enhance program support 　　without signs of any manipulating for personal 　　gain 　Documents showing— 　　• how experts or third parties helped obtain 　　　consensus or support 　　• the minutes from meetings where experts and 　　　third parties were used

3. Uses objectivity to build consensus	Documents showing use of best practices for positive negotiating approaches Example: Being able to influence a stakeholder that seems biased toward a different approach
4. Takes opportunities to capitalize on opportunities to resolve stakeholder issues	Documents showing feedback from stakeholders that the program manager acted in a proactive way Example: The ability to reach out to stakeholders to resolve issues of concern Documents showing feedback from the stakeholders that the program manager acted with self-confidence

5.0　Unit of Competence: Thinking Critically

USING HIGHER-LEVEL, ANALYTICAL, ABSTRACT, AND OPEN THINKING TO FORMULATE QUESTIONS AND ISSUES IN ORDER TO MAKE BETTER DECISIONS

ELEMENT 5.1　CONDUCTS ONGOING ANALYSES TO IDENTIFY TRENDS, VARIANCES, AND ISSUES

PERFORMANCE CRITERIA	TYPES OF EVIDENCE
1. Regularly analyzes program metrics including benefits, cost, schedule, scope, quality, risk, etc. to identify trends, variances, and issues	Examples include: Earned value reports, quality control reports, benefit registers, risk registers, change requests, and other documentation Regular meetings with stakeholders to discuss issues, variances and trends to determine action steps to control or improve performance Crashing the schedule and conducting program and project tasks in an overlapping or concurrent manner Conducting stress tests, destructive tests, or other quality control measures to ensure conformance to specifications Executes and uses contingency plans as required to mitigate impact of risks
2. Continuously scans the program's environment to help understand internal needs, assets, and the overall external environment in which it is operating	Examples include: Using various forms of environmental scanning, to include both internal and external An environment scan report that enumerates: Any trends or events (e.g., scientific, economic, political, etc.) that are important to the program A forecast of potential threats, opportunities, or changes to the program implied by those trends or events Those trends that are speeding up or slowing down, converging or diverging, or interacting in ways that will have an impact on program goals and objectives
3. Monitors stakeholder attitudes and perceptions to ensure their continued support or to thwart negative influences	Examples include: Formal and informal discussions with stakeholders Customer satisfaction surveys of stakeholders Capturing stakeholder attitudes through comments made formally or informally, directly to the program team, or through a third party Documents showing stakeholder survey results and action plans to address any issues

ELEMENT 5.2 APPLIES FACT-BASED DECISION MAKING TO CURRENT AND PROSPECTIVE ISSUES	
PERFORMANCE CRITERIA	TYPES OF EVIDENCE
1. Prepares for decision making by gathering all relevant facts and information	Examples: Accounting reports, earned value management reports, benefit registers, risk registers, commentary from key individuals, reference reports, external sources, and any source of credible data and information Documents showing sources, relevancy, completeness, thoroughness, and accuracy of the information obtained
2. Develops a list of alternative decision approaches and vets with key stakeholders	Examples include: Brainstorming meetings where alternatives are explored Assumptions analysis Using decision-trees, pair-wise comparison, or other decision-making tools Documents showing alternatives under consideration, including positive and negative consequences of each one
3. Makes decisions based on all relevant facts	Examples include: Decision-making meetings where the problem is clearly defined Decision is framed correctly by knowing who is impacted, who needs to provide inputs, who should be part of the discussion, and who should make and review the decision People responsible for implementation are identified and it is determined that they can do it Methods to measure and monitor the results Documents showing meeting minutes enumerating decisions made and their impact
ELEMENT 5.3 WORKS PROACTIVELY WITH THE PROGRAM GOVERNANCE STRUCTURE THAT PROVIDES FOR DECISION MAKING AT THE APPROPRIATE LEVELS	
PERFORMANCE CRITERIA	TYPES OF EVIDENCE
1. Establishes clear rules and guidance as to the decision-making authority of team members and other stakeholders	Documents showing decision-making rules and guidance Examples include: Conducting sessions with the team to review decision-making rules and guidance Communicating to all stakeholders how key decisions will be made, who will make them, and who needs to approve them, if applicable "Signing authority" document for expenditure of funds, contract obligations, and other critical functions

2. Establishes an issue escalation process	Documents showing how issues will be escalated to higher levels in the program or to the Program Governance Board Example: Delegation of authority designations
3. Continuously "pushes down" decision making to the level closest to the issue	Examples include: Actively encouraging team members to make decisions without seeking higher-level approval Providing team members with training or mentoring in decision making Continuously reviewing decisions to see if they were done at the right level in the team, how long it took to make the decision, and the impact of the decision itself Removing those people from the decision-making process who struggle with making a decision, thus negatively impacting program progress Ensuring that the appropriate data and information are available through the program communications and other processes to assist in making fact-based decisions Conducting more meetings that focus on decisions, not discussions

ELEMENT 5.4 *CONSTRUCTIVELY CHALLENGES COMMON BELIEFS AND ASSUMPTIONS—ALWAYS LOOKING FOR A BETTER WAY*

PERFORMANCE CRITERIA	TYPES OF EVIDENCE
1. Engages team members and other stakeholders in spirited discussions on current practices, assumptions, and constraints	Examples include: Standing up to pressure from more senior professionals Taking a clear, firm position in the face of opposition Taking a controversial position to defend an important principle Easily working with executive or C-level executives, key client contacts, and other influential individuals
2. Encourages innovative and creative thinking to solve problems and drive the program forward	Examples include: Soliciting the views of stakeholders in a variety of ways Reaching out to individuals and organizations not associated with the program to obtain dispassionate, third-party views on program direction Requesting reviews/audits from formal and informal sources to uncover problems earlier rather than later Documents showing feedback provided Example: Practicing a policy of "no surprises"

| 3. Focuses on Kaizen, reengineering, and other methods to produce better results in less time with a high degree of customer satisfaction | Example: Maintaining a best practice library to document use of new technologies, techniques, approaches, and methodologies during the program life cycle

Documents showing metrics to demonstrate how process improvement benefited the program

Example: Providing suggestions to the knowledge repository with knowledge assets to share |

6.0　Unit of Competence: Facilitating

ESTABLISHES AN ATMOSPHERE AMONG TEAM MEMBERS AND STAKEHOLDERS TO FACILITATE PROGRAM SUCCESS

ELEMENT 6.1　PLANS FOR SUCCESS FROM THE START OF THE PROGRAM	
PERFORMANCE CRITERIA	TYPES OF EVIDENCE
1. Prepares a high-level plan to guide project and operational managers	Examples include: 　Conducting brainstorming sessions, conducting interviews, using questionnaires and surveys, and building on the business case and the program charter 　Based on feedback, preparing a high-level plan as guidance
2. Sets program milestones in the high-level plan that can be met early in the life cycle	Examples include: 　Following an approach that early success can lead to an atmosphere of later successes among team members 　Providing the team with choices and options in terms of meeting milestones

ELEMENT 6.2　ENSURES THAT ALL TEAM MEMBERS WORK TOGETHER TO ACHIEVE PROGRAM GOALS	
PERFORMANCE CRITERIA	TYPES OF EVIDENCE
1. Promotes a strong team concept to all program members	Examples include: 　Conducting a program kick-off meeting that includes suppliers and vendors 　Stressing the interdependencies between and among component projects 　Promoting the sharing of resources across component projects 　Conducting program review meetings on a regular basis 　Celebrating successes as one program team 　Establishing awards based on team performance rather than individual component performance
2. Successfully gets team members to quickly cooperate, collaborate, and support one another	Examples include: 　Combining team development activities with regular meetings and reviews 　Providing performance incentives for completing program milestones ahead of schedule 　Providing performance incentives for achieving quality requirements at the lowest cost 　Rotating component project managers among various activities, including staff functions of the Program Management Office

	Creating special ad hoc teams to address particular issues of the program (e.g., cost reduction committee) Providing specific training to groups of team members engaged in critical functions Sending specific groups of team members to special conferences and industry events
3. Creates a sense of excitement and enthusiasm for the program among all team members	Examples include: Stressing benefits realization to the organization and ultimate end user of the product(s) or service(s) the program will produce Emphasizing particular skills team members will acquire as a result of working on the program Emphasizing exposure that team members will gain to organization executives, industry leaders, political figures, the press, or other key stakeholders as a result of working on the program Promoting the acquisition of credentials such as the PMP®, PgMP®, MSP®, Prince2®, ITIL®, or other desirable credentials as part of career development on the program

ELEMENT 6.3 EFFECTIVELY RESOLVES ISSUES TO SOLVE PROBLEMS	
PERFORMANCE CRITERIA	TYPES OF EVIDENCE
1. Simplifies complexities for ease of analysis	Example: Listing issues and distributing them to team members and other stakeholders for suggestions Documents showing— • maintenance of issue and action-item logs • proposed actions to results obtained Example: Using techniques to decompose problems
2. Shows persistence and consistency in actions	Documents showing— • feedback from stakeholders regarding approaches used by the program manager • meeting minutes, decision logs, and action-item logs stating decisions made
3. Aggregates multiple, related issues	Documents showing— • the interdependencies between projects and non-project work to easily identify related issues • the findings to show relationships and linkages between issues

4. Observes discrepancies, trends, and interrelationships in program data	Documents showing— • the results of trend analysis • any external changes affecting the program

ELEMENT 6.4 EFFECTIVELY HANDLES PERSONAL AND TEAM ADVERSITY

PERFORMANCE CRITERIA	TYPES OF EVIDENCE
1. Maintains self-control and responds calmly	Examples include: When the program manager had strong emotions but kept them in check to resolve problems objectively Using stress-management approaches to help control responses Documents showing feedback from stakeholders indicating the program manager displayed self-control
2. Admits one's own shortcomings and takes responsibility for actions	Examples include: Recognizing areas that the program manager should focus on for personal improvement Actively listening to constructive feedback Taking responsibility for failure and the need to make revisions to the program
3. Practices a philosophy of learning from mistakes	Documents showing— • feedback from stakeholders that the program manager learned from mistakes • feedback from stakeholders in terms of the program manager's improvements in his or her own personal competencies Example: Self-analysis to understand causes of mistakes and discussions of the results of these analyses with others for feedback

7.0 Unit of Competence: Mentoring	
ENCOURAGES AND FACILITATES TEAM MEMBER PROFESSIONAL DEVELOPMENT	
ELEMENT 7.1 SUPPORTS MENTORING FOR PROGRAM TEAM MEMBERS	
PERFORMANCE CRITERIA	TYPES OF EVIDENCE
1. Models appropriate team, professional, and organizational behavior	Documents showing feedback from stakeholders that the program manager took initiative when required Example: Using effective problem-solving techniques Documents showing feedback from the team on approaches used Example: An issue log with documented resolutions Documents showing— • feedback that the program manager showed consistency in actions and transparency in communications • activities that support both the program and the organizational goals • feedback from stakeholders that the program manager maintained confidentiality
2. Displays a genuine personal interest in team member's performance and development as individuals and as a team	Documents showing the results of a training/development needs analysis after the team is established to see whether additional training is warranted Examples include: Maintaining a high level of motivation among the team given challenges The development of an individual development plan (IDP)
ELEMENT 7.2 ESTABLISHES A FORMAL MENTORING PROGRAM	
PERFORMANCE CRITERIA	TYPES OF EVIDENCE
1. Provides opportunities for both informal and formal mentoring	Documents showing available mentoring programs in the organization Examples include: Providing information on these mentoring programs to team members Encouraging team members to participate in mentoring programs Identifying individuals to serve as mentors from the program, from other units in the organization, or outside the organization Providing training opportunities for those selected as mentors

	Providing opportunities for mentees to participate during the time they are part of the program
	Encouraging the mentor and mentee to establish goals for the relationship
	Documents showing established goals and metrics to assess the effectiveness of mentoring
	Example: Surveys by those in the program as mentors and mentees as to its effectiveness
	Documents showing feedback from survey results and meetings with mentors and mentees
	Examples include:
	Analyzing individual performance to learn from any mistakes or failures and discussing them with the mentor
	Terminating the relationship if it is not proving beneficial
2. Serves as an informal mentor as required	Examples include:
	Reviewing efforts under way by individuals and the team, and providing informal mentoring for overall performance improvement
	Offering input in a casual and indirect manner
	Presentations to demonstrate the importance of the mentoring program to the organization
	Demonstrating skills, behaviors, and attitudes that may assist others
	Offering suggestions, opportunities, and problem-solving approaches as to how issues were handled on previous programs
	Providing opportunities for team members to meet one-on-one to discuss problems and ways to best handle them
	Documents showing—
	• feedback from team members as to the effectiveness of responses
	• feedback that the program manager respected personal, ethnic, and cultural differences

ELEMENT 7.3 SUPPORTS INDIVIDUAL AND TEAM DEVELOPMENT ACTIVITIES	
PERFORMANCE CRITERIA	TYPES OF EVIDENCE

1. Helps team members identify opportunities for professional development	Examples include:
	   Offering suggestions to assist team members in achieving long-term professional goals
	   Providing information regarding the organization's career path in project and program management
	 Documents showing available training opportunities
	 Examples include:
	   Providing information regarding possible training to improve one's competencies in program management
	   Providing opportunities for participation in professional organizations and conferences
	 Documents showing time in the schedule that is provided for professional development opportunities

2. Promotes failures as learning opportunities	Examples include:
	   Feedback that is supportive and informative
	   Feedback that emphasizes development of certain competencies, skills, and knowledge
	 Documents showing—
	   • any changes noted later in the program
	   • lessons learned

3. Establishes an environment of confidence with respect for individual differences	Documents showing feedback from the team that the program manager respected individual differences Example: Creating conditions that motivated and enabled others to do their best
ELEMENT 7.4 RECOGNIZES AND REWARDS INDIVIDUAL AND TEAM ACCOMPLISHMENTS	
PERFORMANCE CRITERIA	TYPES OF EVIDENCE
1. Celebrates success throughout the program	Examples include: Formal recognition of accomplishments by specific individuals and the entire team How the team celebrated achievements Documents showing lessons learned

2. Establishes a system for both team and individual rewards	Documents showing an approach to recognize team accomplishments in addition to those of individuals on the program Example: Recognizing individuals who contributed breakthrough ideas as well as those who provided support in the process Documents showing the team's commitment to a team-based reward and recognition system Examples include: Surveys of performance effectiveness among the team using a 360-degree approach Surveys of team members as to the effectiveness of the system and needed changes
3. Balances individual interests with those of the organization	Documents showing feedback from stakeholders that the program manager and members of his or her team noted distinctions between their own interests and those of the organization

8.0 Unit of Competence: Embracing Change
RECOGNIZES CHANGES WILL AFFECT THE PROGRAM AND IS POSITIVE TOWARD THEIR OCCURRENCE

ELEMENT 8.1 ESTABLISHES AN ENVIRONMENT RECEPTIVE TO CHANGE	
PERFORMANCE CRITERIA	TYPES OF EVIDENCE
1. Recognizes and promotes the change to be introduced to the organization by the program	Example: Meeting with stakeholders to identify the extent of the change and the barriers or obstacles to making change happen Determining and documenting the "change readiness" of the organization Ensuring that the transition plan will be developed early to facilitate the change
2. Recognizes that the life cycle of the program will result in changes	Example: Meeting with stakeholders and team members to set the stage to be prepared for program changes Documents showing— • minutes of meetings held • feedback from stakeholders that the program manager realized change was not to be avoided given the longer life of programs

3. Promotes an approach to change that is positive	Documents showing feedback from stakeholders that the program manager is receptive to change
	Example: Presentations to the team that changes will occur and they may be positive, not negative, to the overall program
	Documents showing feedback from presentations to the team
	Examples include:
	  Providing training opportunities to team members in change management
	  Providing time in the program schedule for team members to study new solutions, situations, tools, and techniques
	  Providing information to team members regarding the organization's approach to change management
	  Meeting with stakeholders to discuss their own tolerance for change on the program
	Documents showing the results from these meetings
	Example: Providing information to team members on the key program stakeholder's tolerance for change

ELEMENT 8.2 INFLUENCES FACTORS THAT MAY RESULT IN CHANGE	
PERFORMANCE CRITERIA	TYPES OF EVIDENCE
1. Identifies factors that could lead to the need for change throughout the program life cycle	Examples include: Surveying stakeholders and conducting interviews to assess in advance any external or internal events that may lead to a change Holding meetings with the Program Governance Board where possible changes are discussed as a routine agenda item Holding meetings with key executives, strategic planners, and members of the portfolio review board or its staff to assess possible changes to the program Documents showing feedback received from these meetings Example: Providing this feedback to the program team
2. Recognizes the need to add an individual skilled in change management to the project team	Example: Suggesting to the Program Governance Board that a person skilled in change management be on the Board and another person with these skills be a member of the program team Documents showing— • feedback received from the Program Governance Board • a change request to update the resource plan Examples include: Analyzing the knowledge, skills, and competency profile of the organization for change management specialists Presentations to the team as to how this individual can assist the team in helping all stakeholders adjust to the change
ELEMENT 8.3 PLANS FOR CHANGE AND ITS POTENTIAL IMPACT	
PERFORMANCE CRITERIA	TYPES OF EVIDENCE
1. Prepares a change management plan	Documents showing— • a change management plan • the feedback from stakeholders regarding the plan • change requests as required to update the plan throughout the program

2. Adapts to changes in the environment to minimize any adverse impact on the program	Documents showing— • feedback from stakeholders that the program manager had an attitude that was positive toward change and could embrace change rather than resist it • change management strategies as part of the change management plan
3. Sets up a part of the program's knowledge repository for changes	Examples include: Encouraging team members to use the program's knowledge repository Encouraging team members to use the EPMO's knowledge repository for lessons learned from previous programs regarding changes and methods and technologies used

ELEMENT 8.4 *MANAGES CHANGES WHEN THEY DO OCCUR*	
PERFORMANCE CRITERIA	TYPES OF EVIDENCE
1. Sets up and follows an integrated change control system for program and project scope changes	Documents showing the contents of the system Examples include: Using change request forms Using change request logs Documents showing— • feedback from stakeholders that the program manager used the system and encouraged the team to follow it • feedback from stakeholders that the program manager demonstrated self-esteem and self-confidence
2. Demonstrates flexibility when changes occur	Documents showing— • feedback that the program manager was flexible toward approaches used to respond to the change, even if a proposed approach was not part of the change management plan • feedback that the program manager viewed changes as opportunities • the results of a change impact analysis Example: Use of change request forms Documents showing— • feedback from stakeholders regarding changes initiated by the program manager • feedback from stakeholders regarding changes facilitated by the program manager

| 3. Assesses interdependencies when changes occur | Documents showing—
• results of impact analysis not on one project in which a change occurred but on other projects or non-project work in the program
• feedback where the program manager proactively resolved problems when a change affected other areas of the program
• feedback from stakeholders that the program manager was action oriented
Example: Use of the knowledge repository for lessons learned based on actions taken |

4

How to Use the Levin-Ward Program Management Complexity Model

Models, per se, have no inherent value unless they are put to use, and put to the test. As practitioners, the authors recognize how important it is to provide practical and pragmatic advice, guidance, and tools to program management professionals, and their organizations, around the world and in all industry sectors. As such, we want to make sure that our competency model can be—and is—used in multiple ways with the specific goal of helping people and organizations improve their ability to manage programs and program complexity.

We have developed three questionnaires—surveys if you will—that the reader can use to compare their individual knowledge and practice, and their organization's practice in program management, with the specific objective of doing things better. We have one questionnaire found in Appendix A for organizations; our questionnaire in Appendix B is for practicing program managers; and the third questionnaire in Appendix C is for prospective program managers. Each one is designed to assess program management capabilities from a different perspective. Taken together, they represent a fairly comprehensive picture of program management capability within an organization.

While we do not claim or represent that our model is perfect, or that the use of our model will guarantee success in all aspects of program management, we can confidently say that it will cause you and your organization to think differently about the way individuals practice program management, and about the environment the organization has established to foster excellence therein, so that a roadmap of improvement can be drawn. Let's first take a look at how organizations can use the model.

Use by Organizations

Overview

The challenges each organization faces in its industry will affect the challenges faced by its program and project managers and the competencies they need to respond to these challenges. However, developing specific, detailed, and unique competencies takes time and can be very expensive. Our model approaches program management at a high level. We have identified competencies that most programs and program managers use most of the time. In short, we assert that there are more similarities regarding competencies in program management across industries than there are differences. To the extent you may want to add some specific ones for your environment, please feel free to do so.

Our model is designed in a way that tailoring it can be easily done by an organization, especially in terms of the documented evidence to show that the competency is practiced by the program manager. While we have used terminology for the evidence from the PMI (2008d), each organization may use different terms for the various plans and reports that are part of its program management methodology. Further, we recognize that many of the desired competencies may need to be learned while on the job, especially in the performance competencies, and evaluated over time to determine improvements. Many of the personal competencies will be based on the characteristics of working with a specific program team and the team members' level of experience in program management along with the program manager's personal characteristics. Other personal competencies will depend on the type of stakeholders involved in the program and their levels of interest and influence over it. For many, one's personal competencies may dictate their ability to manage a highly complex program versus one that is lower in complexity.

Process improvement of any type is never an easy undertaking and requires support and commitment at all levels. Changes are difficult, and often are resisted; however, with the increase in program management in organizations, more people with the needed competencies for success are required as the talent gap primarily focuses on the project manager and not the program manager. Experienced program managers, however, are required for program and organizational success. These managers then can mentor prospective program managers with an emphasis at all levels, from learning from mistakes and improving competencies through such learning. It is a relatively easy process to hire people who on paper appear to have the talent to manage a complex program; the difficulty lies in ensuring that the program managers in the organization can build the necessary relationships at all levels, communicate effectively, develop trust quickly, and lead and motivate a team. The focus required is to be able to recognize, coordinate, and maximize interdependencies on the program, solving problems, and resolving issues effectively and efficiently.

At the organizational level, support for the competency model cannot be understated. The executives must describe the model's objectives and why it is needed, focusing on respect for program managers and the organization's investment in its staff members. It must be viewed as a method for continuous improvement and not as something that is used in personnel performance evaluation for such things as raises or promotions. Furthermore, it cannot be viewed in the organization as a one-time exercise or the "fad of the month." Executive commitment for its implementation, and defined roles and responsibilities, are needed. Executives must encourage their program managers to see the model as a way to help them achieve objectives and personal development in the field.

This means that executives must lead the way in making sure people within the organization understand its objectives and why it is pursuing certain programs and projects over others. These strategic objectives then can be tied to the improvement initiative in overall competencies in the program management field. Executive support then will lead to support from the current and prospective program managers in the organization.

To be sure, implementation of the model, beginning with questionnaires, is a project in itself. It must be planned, managed, and communicated as to its importance. It requires a sponsor and a project manager, with a detailed plan and metrics to monitor the overall use of the model and, more importantly, to determine whether or not it has been accepted and is being used.

We suggest that you start by doing the following.

Program Management Organizational Assessment

Use the questionnaire in Appendix A to conduct an Organizational Assessment of program management. It is divided into two sections: There are 62 number of questions related to program management performance competencies and 35 number of questions regarding the personal competencies of the collective body of program managers within the organization. Scores can be calculated on the individual components of performance competencies and personal competencies. So, for example, you can see the extent to which your organization practices Monitoring and Controlling competencies as compared to the Model; or how your organization's program managers collectively score on Leading. Additionally, you will be able to calculate a total score for the Performance Competencies and a total score for the Personal Competencies.

There is no pass/fail. The scores are simply an indicator of where your organization falls on a continuum of practice of competencies identified in the model. That said, it is not unlikely that an organization will have stronger practices in one area than in others. By noting which areas are weakest, an improvement roadmap can then be established to address the weaker areas first. However, a total score in each area will give a general view of the collective practice of program management across the board.

The questionnaire should be distributed to as many people as possible throughout the organization who have knowledge of the practice of program management. In addition to the program managers themselves, it should be distributed to business unit heads and directors, team members from all functional departments, project managers, EPMO staff, clients (both internal and external), suppliers, vendors, employees, and other interested parties. The questionnaire should also be expanded, based on your unique needs, to collect certain qualifying information such as name, business unit, location, cost center, and any other designation that can be used to sort the data for reporting purposes. For example, in a multinational corporation (MNC), it would be interesting to compare the scores for various geographies, business units, or regions. We once worked with an MNC in the technology industry that conducted a global survey and noted that risk management, for example, was not practiced with any consistency in one part of the world, whereas in others it was firmly established. This organization was then able to relate lower customer satisfaction ratings in this area to poor risk management practices. With an increased emphasis on risk management in this particular geography, spearheaded by the PMO, customer satisfaction ratings improved coincident with the rise in better risk management practices.

Guidelines

When the model is used for an organizational assessment, the following guidelines are suggested for its implementation.

Use the model, and its questionnaire, to determine a baseline of current competencies of program managers in the organization to determine areas of strength and areas in need of improvement. Recognize any development needs if performance does not meet the criteria set forth in the model. Also recognize areas of strength that the program manager can impart to others. If the model is used across the organization or at a business unit or department level, provide a log of the findings.

In addition, when new programs are selected, the results from the model can help match the program manager to a new position as well as his or her team members as the requirements of the program can be linked to the competencies possessed by the program manager. The model can improve how personnel resources are used throughout the organization. Having competent program managers with leadership competencies and program managers that stress working with stakeholders and building relationships, these individuals can better recognize the interdependencies between the projects on the program and their relationship to overall corporate strategy; chances are they will also be better suited for managing and motivating the program team.

The model also can be used during the hiring process to see if the potential staff members have the desired competencies for the organization's programs. They can follow the questions in the model for prospective program managers.

Additionally, program sponsors can review the program manager's use of the model and subsequent improvements based on items in his or her performance plan.

Use by Program Managers

Overview

Program managers must view the competency model not as a one-time exercise but as a way to periodically assess whether they continue to improve in their own overall competencies in program management. First, they should use the model to establish a baseline as to where they stand in terms of both the performance and personal competencies. From this baseline, the next step is to develop a personal improvement or action plan focusing on those that they believe are the most significant. To prepare this plan, program managers should consider seeking advice from their manager, sponsor, customers, and even their team. They may wish to involve a mentor for assistance.

With improved competencies, overall performance should improve, therein reducing stress in the complexity of leading a program and reducing the need to be a hero in order to deliver the program's benefits. By using the model at scheduled intervals to see if improvements have been made, program managers can focus on the next set of competencies for greater enhancements, documenting progress in their performance plan. No doubt overall job satisfaction should improve as well.

Program Manager Assessment

Use the questionnaire found in Appendix B to conduct an assessment of the program managers in the organization. Again, there are 62 questions related to program management performance competencies and 35 questions regarding the personal competencies. Our intent was to provide a questionnaire that a program manager could complete based on his or her program to see the extent to which performance and personal competencies are practiced. As a self-assessment, it provides the program manager with keen insight as to where he or she needs to focus to help increase the chance of success of the program. As is the case of the Organizational Program Management Assessment, it is not a pass/fail instrument.

Some program managers, or organizations, may wish to rephrase the first few words of every question so that others may also complete the instrument so it can be used as a "multi-rater" instrument. For example, for Element 1.1 we write, "I know my program has identified...." This is the questionnaire the program manager would use, but when issued to others for multi-rater purposes, the question would be written as "The program manager has identified...." By doing this, you will be able to see how the program manager describes his or her performance, but you will also be able to see how others perceive the program manager's level of practice in these competencies.

Great care must be exercised, however, when using this as a multi-rater. The authors do not suggest or condone the use of a multi-rater as an official personnel evaluation for compensation or other personnel decisions. A multi-rater should be used solely for developmental purposes.

In addition to its possible use as a multi-rater instrument, we suggest that you aggregate the individual program manager's results into one "collective" report of scores. By doing so, you will be able to see the relative strengths and weaknesses of the body of program managers who completed the survey. By employing various demographic information identifying survey participants, you will be able to compare scores across business units, divisions, geographies, functional specializations, and the like. Such comparisons can highlight or isolate areas of strong performance as well as areas where immediate intervention is required.

Guidelines

After the assessment, discuss the results with the program manager as soon as possible. Develop a competency development plan for the program manager, working in conjunction with the individual, with specific, measurable activities and a timetable recognizing that not every item can be done at once. Address improvements through a variety of approaches. Use this plan in a proactive way to determine the best approach to overcome any gaps in a timely manner, focusing on individual goals and objectives and those areas in need of greatest improvement.

Execute the plan and reassess performance periodically, approximately every six to twelve months. Assess as well the approach that was followed to address the needed competency for its effectiveness.

Encourage feedback as to the effectiveness of the model. Note any continuous improvement as it relates to individual and team performance. Continuously assess its effectiveness by seeing whether the desired outcomes are being realized.

Use by Prospective Program Managers

Program management differs from the management of a single project or even multiple projects. Often, if one is managing multiple projects, even though they may have the same client or use some of the same resources, it is not the same as managing a program. Benefits realization, resource allocation and project prioritization can be handled much differently in the program environment. For example, the projects may not have similar objectives but may have interdependencies between them. The complexities are far greater than just the need to focus one's time on one project and then to focus time on another project if one is managing multiple projects but not as a program. Further, one's own ability to be proactive and flexible is notable for overall success.

Prospective program managers can benefit from the model. Their answers to specific questions may help to determine whether or not they will wish to be candidates for program management positions. Organizations can also use this questionnaire to help evaluate prospective candidates.

Prospective Program Manager Assessment

The third questionnaire, found in Appendix C, is more along the lines of an "exam." We recognize that the more organizations become involved in program management, the greater the need to identify personnel who have the potential of becoming competent program managers. To assist in this process, we have worded the questions in a way that forms a multiple-choice exam in an attempt to gauge the level of knowledge an individual has about program management practices.

The score of this exam will provide individuals with an indication of where they need to improve their knowledge in program management. After all, knowledge is the first step in competency development, but only the first step. The correct answers are found in Appendix C1.

A word of caution: Just because an individual may score very high on this questionnaire does not, in and of itself, indicate that this person would be a highly competent program manager. Accordingly, it is not to be used as a "hiring" tool by the organization. Knowledge must be applied, and it is in the application of knowledge where competency is demonstrated. That said, if knowledge is lacking, it is difficult to imagine a scenario in which the person could possibly make a competent program manager even if the desire to be one was very strong. Think of it this way: Just because someone might want to be a neurosurgeon does not make them one without knowledge *and* practice!

Appendix A: Questions for Organizations

The following questions are designed for use by organizational leaders in determining the overall knowledge, skills, and competencies of the program managers in the organization.

Each question relates to one of the domains in the model and is scored using a Likert scale as follows:

1 = Not followed in our organization
2 = Practiced by less than half of our program managers
3 = Practiced by about 50% of our program managers
4 = Practiced by about 75% of our program managers
5 = Practiced by more than 90% of our program managers

First, the following questions refer to the performance competencies.

1.0 Defining the Program					

ELEMENT: 1.1 STRATEGIC BENEFITS OF THE PROGRAM ARE UNDERSTOOD BY ALL STAKEHOLDERS

	1	2	3	4	5
1. We identify the high-level benefits of each of our programs, which are distributed to our stakeholders.					

ELEMENT 1.2 A PLAN TO INITIATE THE PROGRAM IS PREPARED

	1	2	3	4	5
2. We develop a high-level plan for our programs to show how the program's objectives align with our organizational objectives.					

ELEMENT 1.3 THE PROGRAM'S OBJECTIVES ARE ALIGNED WITH STRATEGIC THE GOALS OF THE ORGANIZATION

	1	2	3	4	5
3. We prepare a strategic directive to describe high-level program goals.					

ELEMENT 1.4 A HIGH-LEVEL BUSINESS CASE IS DEVELOPED FOR THE PROGRAM

	1	2	3	4	5
4. We prepare a high-level business case that we use to note program benefits, the need for the program, its feasibility, and justification.					

ELEMENT 1.5 A NUMBER OF GATES OR STAGES ARE IDENTIFIED WHEN PROGRAM STATUS (INCLUDING BENEFITS REALIZATION) WILL BE REVIEWED

	1	2	3	4	5
5. We establish a governance structure with stage gate reviews for our programs.					
TOTAL – DEFINING THE PROGRAM					

2.0 Initiating the Program					

ELEMENT 2.1 A PROGRAM CHARTER IS PREPARED

	1	2	3	4	5
1. We have a charter for each program that defines in more detail how the program will be set up and managed.					

ELEMENT 2.2 THE PROGRAM VISION IS DOCUMENTED TO DESCRIBE THE END STATE AND ITS BENEFIT TO THE ORGANIZATION

	1	2	3	4	5
2. We have a defined vision for each program.					

ELEMENT 2.3 KEY PROGRAM DECISION MAKERS ARE IDENTIFIED

	1	2	3	4	5
3. We identify the Executive Sponsor and Program Manager, along with other members of the Program's Governance Board.					

ELEMENT 2.4 STAKEHOLDER EXPECTATIONS AND INTERESTS ARE IDENTIFIED					
	1	2	3	4	5
4. We document an initial list of stakeholders and a preliminary stakeholder management strategy.					

ELEMENT 2.5 HIGH-LEVEL RISKS TO THE PROGRAM ARE IDENTIFIED					
	1	2	3	4	5
5. We prepare and analyze potential high-level risks to our programs.					

ELEMENT 2.6 CANDIDATE PROJECTS TO BE IN THE PROGRAM, AS WELL AS NON-PROJECT WORK, ARE IDENTIFIED					
	1	2	3	4	5
6. We prepare criteria to use for projects and non-project work to be part of each of our programs.					

ELEMENT 2.7 AN INITIAL INFRASTRUCTURE FOR PROGRAM MANAGEMENT IS DETERMINED					
	1	2	3	4	5
7. We determine whether we need a new organization for each program and any required support systems.					

ELEMENT 2.8 THE TIMETABLE TO COMPLETE THE PROGRAM IS DETERMINED					
	1	2	3	4	5
8. We prepare a high-level schedule for our programs before they begin.					

ELEMENT 2.9 INITIAL ESTIMATES OF THE PROGRAM'S COST ARE PREPARED					
	1	2	3	4	5
9. We set up funding goals for each of our programs as part of an overall financial framework.					

ELEMENT 2.10 KEY RESOURCES FOR PROGRAM MANAGEMENT ARE IDENTIFIED TO SET UP THE PROGRAM					
	1	2	3	4	5
10. We prepare a list of the key resources that we believe we need for each program before it begins.					

ELEMENT 2.11 THE PROGRAM CHARTER IS APPROVED					
	1	2	3	4	5
11. We formally approve the charter for each of our programs.					
TOTAL – INITIATING					

3.0 Planning the Program

ELEMENT 3.1 A PROGRAM MANAGEMENT PLAN IS PREPARED					
	1	2	3	4	5
1. We prepare a program management plan for each of our programs.					

ELEMENT 3.2 A BENEFITS REALIZATION PLAN IS PREPARED

	1	2	3	4	5
2. We prepare a benefits realization plan for each of our programs.					

ELEMENT 3.3 KEY PROGRAM RISKS AND ISSUES ARE IDENTIFIED

	1	2	3	4	5
3. We prepare a risk management plan for each of our programs.					

ELEMENT 3.4 THE PROGRAM'S BUDGET IS DETERMINED

	1	2	3	4	5
4. We prepare a financial management framework with an initial program budget for each of our programs.					

ELEMENT 3.5 DEPENDENCIES, CONSTRAINTS, AND ASSUMPTIONS ARE DOCUMENTED

	1	2	3	4	5
5. We document the boundaries of our programs by preparing a program scope statement.					

ELEMENT 3.6 A STRATEGY TO MANAGE THE PROGRAM AND ITS COMPONENTS IS AGREED UPON AND DOCUMENTED

	1	2	3	4	5
6. We document the interdependencies among the projects and non-project work in our programs.					

ELEMENT 3.7 NECESSARY FEASIBILITY STUDIES ARE CONDUCTED

	1	2	3	4	5
7. We recognize that programs represent change based on internal and external events.					

ELEMENT 3.8 A ROADMAP OR ARCHITECTURE TO SHOW THE INTER-RELATIONSHIPS AMONG THE COMPONENT PROJECTS AND NON-PROJECT WORK IN THE PROGRAM IS PREPARED

	1	2	3	4	5
8. We update our initial roadmap reflecting program changes.					

ELEMENT 3.9 A COMMUNICATIONS STRATEGY FOR EACH KEY STAKEHOLDER IS DETERMINED

	1	2	3	4	5
9. We document a stakeholder management strategy on our programs.					

ELEMENT 3.10 A PROGRAM MANAGEMENT OFFICE (PMO) IS APPROVED AND IMPLEMENTED

	1	2	3	4	5
10. We establish a PMO for each of our programs.					

ELEMENT 3.11 TOOLS, PROCESSES, AND TECHNIQUES REQUIRED FOR PROGRAM MANAGEMENT ARE OBTAINED

	1	2	3	4	5
11. We establish a Program Management Information System for each of our programs.					

ELEMENT 3.12 THE PROGRAM MANAGEMENT PLAN IS APPROVED

	1	2	3	4	5
12. We follow a formal process to approve each program's management plan.					

ELEMENT 3.13 A PROGRAM MANAGEMENT GOVERNANCE STRUCTURE IS DETERMINED

	1	2	3	4	5
13. We establish a Governance Board for each program.					

ELEMENT 3.14 A PROGRAM CONTROL FRAMEWORK IS ESTABLISHED TO ASSIST IN BENEFIT MEASUREMENT AS WELL AS IN OVERALL MANAGEMENT OF THE PROGRAM'S COMPONENTS

	1	2	3	4	5
14. We follow a program management methodology on our programs.					
TOTAL – PLANNING					

4.0 Executing the Program

ELEMENT 4.1 PROJECTS ARE INITIATED AS PART OF THE PROGRAM

	1	2	3	4	5
1. We follow a formal process to initiate each project that is part of a program.					

ELEMENT 4.2 SHARED RESOURCES REQUIRED FOR COMPONENT PROJECTS IN THE PROGRAM AND THE NON-PROJECT WORK ARE COORDINATED

	1	2	3	4	5
2. We follow a process to determine any resource issues on our program to easily resolve them.					

ELEMENT 4.3 CHANGE REQUESTS ARE REVIEWED

	1	2	3	4	5
3. We follow a documented change control process on our programs.					

ELEMENT 4.4 ADDITIONAL WORK IS AUTHORIZED AS REQUIRED

	1	2	3	4	5
4. We follow a documented decision-making process when there are changes to the projects and non-project work in our program.					

ELEMENT 4.5 COMMUNICATIONS WITH STAKEHOLDERS IS FOSTERED AND ENCOURAGED AT ALL LEVELS					
	1	2	3	4	5
5. We work to ensure each stakeholder has the information he or she requires concerning our programs.					

ELEMENT 4.6 COMMUNICATIONS WITH MEMBERS OF THE PROGRAM GOVERNANCE BOARD OCCURS ON A REGULAR BASIS					
	1	2	3	4	5
6. We hold regularly scheduled meetings with the members of the Program Governance Board on each of our programs.					

ELEMENT 4.7 ALIGNMENT OF THE PROGRAM'S GOALS, AND ITS BENEFITS, IS ASSESSED AGAINST THAT OF THE ORGANIZATION					
	1	2	3	4	5
7. We document the link between strategic goals of our organization to our programs and their projects.					

ELEMENT 4.8 COMMON ACTIVITIES AMONG THE PROGRAM'S PROJECTS AND NON-PROJECT WORK ARE COORDINATED					
	1	2	3	4	5
8. We provide guidelines to project managers who are working on a program to better manage interrelationships.					

ELEMENT 4.9 DEPENDENCIES WITH OTHER ORGANIZATIONAL INITIATIVES ARE COORDINATED					
	1	2	3	4	5
9. We use a knowledge management system to document dependencies between our programs and other initiatives under way in the organization.					

ELEMENT 4.10 THE PROGRAM MANAGEMENT PLAN IS EXECUTED					
	1	2	3	4	5
10. We follow the program management plan on our programs.					
TOTAL – EXECUTING					

5.0 Monitoring and Controlling the Program					

ELEMENT 5.1 PROGRESS IS ANALYZED ACCORDING TO THE PROGRAM MANAGEMENT PLAN					
	1	2	3	4	5
1. We regularly review programs to see if schedule milestones and budget goals are met.					

ELEMENT 5.2 BENEFIT REALIZATION IS ANALYZED ACCORDING TO THE BENEFITS REALIZATION PLAN

	1	2	3	4	5
2. We analyze our progress in realizing the program's benefits according to the benefits realization plan.					

ELEMENT 5.3 ISSUES AND RISKS ARE CONTINUOUSLY IDENTIFIED, AND CORRECTIVE ACTIONS ARE TAKEN AS REQUIRED

	1	2	3	4	5
3. We follow a continual process to identify risks and issues to resolve them effectively.					

ELEMENT 5.4 EXTERNAL ENVIRONMENTAL CHANGES ARE ANALYZED TO DETERMINE THE POSSIBLE IMPACT ON THE PROGRAM AND ITS REALIZATION OF BENEFITS

	1	2	3	4	5
4. We follow a process to identify the effect of external changes on our programs and their overall direction.					

ELEMENT 5.5 GOVERNANCE OVERSIGHT IS REGULARLY PRACTICED AT THE PROGRAM AND PROJECT LEVELS

	1	2	3	4	5
5. We follow a process of taking corrective and preventive actions based on feedback by the Program Governance Boards.					

ELEMENT 5.6 PROGRAM CHANGES ARE IMPLEMENTED IN ACCORDANCE WITH ESTABLISHED INTEGRATED CHANGE CONTROL PROCEDURES

	1	2	3	4	5
6. We use integrated change control system in our programs.					

ELEMENT 5.7 PROGRAM EXECUTION IS MONITORED ACCORDING TO THE PROGRAM MANAGEMENT PLAN

	1	2	3	4	5
7. We use the program management plan to monitor actual execution of the program.					

ELEMENT 5.8 SCHEDULE SLIPPAGES AND OPPORTUNITIES ARE IDENTIFIED AND MANAGED

	1	2	3	4	5
8. We follow the program's schedule and use metrics to assist in monitoring and control.					

ELEMENT 5.9 PROACTIVE COST CONTROL IS PRACTICED

	1	2	3	4	5
9. We follow the program's financial plan and use a cost management system on our programs.					

ELEMENT 5.10 STAKEHOLDER EXPECTATIONS ARE MANAGED					
	1	2	3	4	5
10. We monitor stakeholder participation on our programs following our stakeholder management strategy.					

ELEMENT 5.11 PERFORMANCE DATA ARE CONSOLIDATED TO DETERMINE APPROPRIATE RESOURCE USE TO DELIVER BENEFITS					
	1	2	3	4	5
11. We follow a process to consolidate data on our programs with regular reporting to monitor resource use and benefit delivery.					

ELEMENT 5.12 COMPONENTS TRANSITION TO CLOSURE					
	1	2	3	4	5
12. We follow a formal process to close each project and non-project work on our programs with sign-offs to show approval.					
TOTAL – MONITORING AND CONTROLLING					

6.0 Closing the Program

ELEMENT 6.1 THE PROGRAM IS FORMALLY CLOSED					
	1	2	3	4	5
1. We follow a process to obtain formal acceptance that the program is officially closed.					

ELEMENT 6.2 PRODUCTS AND SERVICES TRANSITION TO OPERATIONS					
	1	2	3	4	5
2. We transition the work of our programs to our customers, users, or an operational or product support unit.					

ELEMENT 6.3 PROGRAM BENEFITS ARE REALIZED					
	1	2	3	4	5
3. We evaluate the planned benefits with the realized benefits with our stakeholders on our programs.					

ELEMENT 6.4 CUSTOMER SUPPORT IS PROVIDED (AS APPLICABLE, SUCH AS DEFINED IN A CONTRACT)					
	1	2	3	4	5
4. We provide customer support as defined in our program management plan on our programs.					

ELEMENT 6.5 LESSONS LEARNED ARE INTEGRATED INTO THE ORGANIZATION'S KNOWLEDGE MANAGEMENT SYSTEM					
	1	2	3	4	5
5. We incorporate lessons learned from each of our programs into our knowledge management system.					
ELEMENT 6.6 FEEDBACK IS PROVIDED ON AREAS OUTSIDE THE PROGRAM					
	1	2	3	4	5
6. We provide feedback on possible improvements in our program management practice that we observe as our programs are completed.					
ELEMENT 6.7 PROGRAM DOCUMENTS ARE ARCHIVED FOR FUTURE REUSE					
	1	2	3	4	5
7. We follow a process to archive the documents prepared on our programs.					
ELEMENT 6.8 CONTRACTUAL OBLIGATIONS ARE MET					
	1	2	3	4	5
8. We review all the contracts on our programs to ensure that contractual obligations are met.					
ELEMENT 6.9 INTELLECTUAL PROPERTY IS CAPTURED FOR REUSE					
	1	2	3	4	5
9. We recognize the importance of reusing intellectual property on future programs considering any legal constraints.					
ELEMENT 6.10 A LEGACY OF BENEFIT SUSTAINMENT IS ACHIEVED					
	1	2	3	4	5
10. We verify that our programs have led to added value to our customers and end users.					
TOTAL – CLOSING					
TOTAL – ALL PERFORMANCE COMPETENCIES					

These questions involve the personal competencies.

1.0 Communicating					
ELEMENT: 1.1 ACTIVELY LISTENS, UNDERSTANDS, AND RESPONDS TO STAKEHOLDERS					
	1	2	3	4	5
1. Our program managers can describe the strategic benefits of their programs to stakeholders at all levels.					
ELEMENT 1.2 USES THE KEY CHANNELS OF COMMUNICATIONS					
	1	2	3	4	5
2. Our program managers regularly and effectively engage customers, sponsors, and project managers through both formal and informal communications.					
ELEMENT 1.3 ENSURES THE QUALITY OF THE INFORMATION THAT IS COMMUNICATED					
	1	2	3	4	5
3. Our program managers provide consistent messages that are accurate and factual to their stakeholders.					
ELEMENT 1.4 TAILORS THE INFORMATION TO THE AUDIENCE					
	1	2	3	4	5
4. Our program managers use different methods to communicate with different stakeholders or stakeholder groups.					
ELEMENT 1.5 EFFECTIVELY USES EACH OF THE DIFFERENT COMMUNICATIONS DIMENSIONS					
	1	2	3	4	5
5. Our program managers recognize their own communications barriers and use different types of communications skills based on the specific program stakeholders involved.					
TOTAL – COMMUNICATING					
2.0 Unit of Competence: Leading					
ELEMENT 2.1 IMPLEMENTS THE PROGRAM'S VISION					
	1	2	3	4	5
1. Our program managers reinforce the vision of the program throughout its life cycle to its stakeholders.					
ELEMENT 2.2 ESTABLISHES THE PROGRAM'S DIRECTION					
	1	2	3	4	5
2. Our program managers follow a program roadmap and use documented critical success factors.					

ELEMENT 2.3 RECOGNIZES THE INTERDEPENDENCIES WITHIN THE PROGRAM

	1	2	3	4	5
3. Our program managers realize how each project in the program and any non-project work relate to one another.					

ELEMENT 2.4 TAKES CALCULATED RISKS: IS VENTURESOME

	1	2	3	4	5
4. Our program managers recognize their level of authority and know when to escalate risks and issues to the Program Governance Board or other groups for resolution.					

ELEMENT 2.5 ASSUMES OWNERSHIP FOR THE PROGRAM

	1	2	3	4	5
5. Our program managers assume full ownership for the program.					
TOTAL – LEADING					

3.0 Unit of Competence: Building Relationships

ELEMENT 3.1 BUILDS TRUST AMONG STAKEHOLDERS, CLIENTS, AND TEAM MEMBERS

	1	2	3	4	5
1. Our program managers act promptly on stakeholder concerns and promote a "win-win" attitude between and among stakeholder groups.					

ELEMENT 3.2 LEVERAGES THE ORGANIZATION'S POLITICAL DYNAMICS TO PROMOTE PROGRAM GOALS

	1	2	3	4	5
2. Our program managers recognize the organization's internal dynamics and work to obtain support from the right people for suggestions for program direction.					

ELEMENT 3.3 ADVOCATES FOR DIVERSITY AND TREATS OTHERS WITH COURTESY AND RESPECT

	1	2	3	4	5
3. Our program managers build a diverse team and provide equal treatment to all individuals.					

ELEMENT 3.4 ESTABLISHES AND DEMONSTRATES HIGH STANDARDS FOR PERSONAL AND TEAM MEMBER PERFORMANCE

	1	2	3	4	5
4. Our program managers establish program and individual performance goals that are realistic and attainable.					

ELEMENT 3.5 PROMOTES AND DEMONSTRATES ETHICS, INTEGRITY, AND ADHERENCE TO CORPORATE VALUES IN ALL INTERACTIONS					
	1	2	3	4	5
5. Our program managers work to promote integrity and to enforce the organization's ethics code and procedures.					
TOTAL – BUILDING RELATIONSHIPS					

4.0 Unit of Competence: Negotiating

ELEMENT 4.1 OBTAINS NEEDED PROGRAM RESOURCES					
	1	2	3	4	5
1. Our program managers use a variety of approaches to obtain the resources they need on their programs.					

ELEMENT 4.2 ENSURES PROGRAM ALIGNMENT WITH THE ORGANIZATION'S STRATEGIES					
	1	2	3	4	5
2. Our program managers recognize the changing organizational priorities and work to ensure continual program alignment.					

ELEMENT 4.3 WORKS PROACTIVELY WITH THE PROGRAM GOVERNANCE BOARD					
	1	2	3	4	5
3. Our program managers regularly seek opinions from the Program Governance Board concerning program direction and work to meet commitments they make to the Board.					

ELEMENT 4.4 PROMOTES OVERALL STAKEHOLDER SUPPORT					
	1	2	3	4	5
4. Our program managers work to maximize any opportunities to promote stakeholder support for their programs.					
TOTAL – NEGOTIATING					

5.0 Unit of Competence: Thinking Critically

ELEMENT 5.1 CONDUCTS ONGOING ANALYSES TO IDENTIFY TRENDS, VARIANCES, AND ISSUES					
	1	2	3	4	5
1. Our program managers evaluate the program environment regularly and monitor stakeholder attitudes and perceptions for any negative influences.					

ELEMENT 5.2 APPLIES FACT-BASED DECISION MAKING TO CURRENT AND PROSPECTIVE ISSUES					
	1	2	3	4	5
2. Our program managers prepare for the decisions they make and base them as much as possible on facts, discussing them as needed with key stakeholders.					

ELEMENT 5.3 WORKS PROACTIVELY WITH THE PROGRAM GOVERNANCE STRUCTURE THAT PROVIDES FOR DECISION MAKING AT THE APPROPRIATE LEVELS

	1	2	3	4	5
3. Our program managers empower others to make decisions as appropriate but escalate issues as required, such as to the Program Governance Board.					

ELEMENT 5.4 CONSTRUCTIVELY CHALLENGES COMMON BELIEFS AND ASSUMPTIONS—ALWAYS LOOKING FOR A BETTER WAY

	1	2	3	4	5
4. Our program managers encourage innovative and creative thinking and strive to achieve results as quickly as possible, promoting a high degree of customer satisfaction.					
TOTAL – THINKING CRITICALLY					

6.0 Unit of Competence: Facilitating

ELEMENT 6.1 PLANS FOR SUCCESS FROM THE START OF THE PROGRAM

	1	2	3	4	5
1. Our program managers establish an environment for their teams that focuses on early successes.					

ELEMENT 6.2 ENSURES THAT ALL TEAM MEMBERS WORK TOGETHER TO ACHIEVE PROGRAM GOALS

	1	2	3	4	5
2. Our program managers conduct kick-off meetings and get team members to quickly cooperate, collaborate, and support one another.					

ELEMENT 6.3 EFFECTIVELY RESOLVES ISSUES TO SOLVE PROBLEMS

	1	2	3	4	5
3. Our program managers work to identify and monitor issues by observing discrepancies, trends, and interrelationships within their programs.					

ELEMENT 6.4 EFFECTIVELY HANDLES PERSONAL AND TEAM ADVERSITY

	1	2	3	4	5
4. Our program managers use self-control and take responsibility for their actions, accepting constructive feedback.					
TOTAL – FACILITATING					

7.0 Unit of Competence: Mentoring

ELEMENT 7.1 SUPPORTS MENTORING FOR TEAM MEMBERS ON THE PROGRAM

	1	2	3	4	5
1. Our program managers model behavior for team members to follow displaying a genuine interest in each team member's performance.					

ELEMENT 7.2 ESTABLISHES A FORMAL MENTORING PROGRAM

	1	2	3	4	5
2. Our program managers provide opportunities for team members to participate if desired in formal and/or informal mentoring programs.					

ELEMENT 7.3 SUPPORTS INDIVIDUAL AND TEAM DEVELOPMENT ACTIVITIES

	1	2	3	4	5
3. Our program managers work with their team members to promote individual and team development.					

ELEMENT 7.4 RECOGNIZES AND REWARDS INDIVIDUAL AND TEAM ACCOMPLISHMENTS

	1	2	3	4	5
4. Our program managers set up approaches to recognize both individual and team accomplishments.					
TOTAL – MENTORING					

8.0 Unit of Competence: Embraces Changes					

ELEMENT 8.1 ESTABLISHES AN ENVIRONMENT RECEPTIVE TO CHANGE

	1	2	3	4	5
1. Our program managers recognize the positive aspects of change and communicate them to program stakeholders.					

ELEMENT 8.2 INFLUENCES FACTORS THAT MAY RESULT IN CHANGE

	1	2	3	4	5
2. Our program managers assess in advance events that may lead to a change on their programs.					

ELEMENT 8.3 PLANS FOR CHANGE AND ITS POTENTIAL IMPACT

	1	2	3	4	5
3. Our program managers adapt to changes in the environment to minimize any adverse impacts on the program.					

ELEMENT 8.4 MANAGES CHANGES WHEN THEY DO OCCUR

	1	2	3	4	5
4. Our program managers demonstrate flexibility when changes occur to make sure the change is viewed positively by the program's team members and other stakeholders.					
TOTAL – EMBRACING CHANGE					
TOTAL – ALL PERSONAL COMPETENCIES					

Appendix B: Questions for Program Managers

The following questions are designed for program managers who wish to assess their own competencies in program management with an emphasis on using the results for their own personal improvement.

In answering the questions, a five-point Likert scale is used as follows:

1 = This practice does not apply to my work
2 = This practice applies to my work less than 25% of the time
3 = This practice applies to my work between 25 and 50% of the time
4 = This practice applies to my work between 50 and 75% of the time
5 = This practice applies to my work more than 75% of the time

1.0 Defining the Program					
ELEMENT: 1.1 STRATEGIC BENEFITS OF THE PROGRAM ARE UNDERSTOOD BY ALL STAKEHOLDERS					
	1	2	3	4	5
1. I know my program has identified at a high-level its expected benefits from the time before the program is proposed to be part of my organization's portfolio.					
ELEMENT 1.2 A PLAN TO INITIATE THE PROGRAM IS PREPARED					
	1	2	3	4	5
2. I recognize that before a program receives initial approval in my organization, a high-level plan is prepared to describe why the program is required.					
ELEMENT 1.3 THE PROGRAM'S OBJECTIVES ARE ALIGNED WITH THE STRATEGIC GOALS OF THE ORGANIZATION					
	1	2	3	4	5
3. I understand the selection criteria my organization uses to select programs and projects, and I know where my program fits in terms of our overall portfolio.					
ELEMENT 1.4 A HIGH-LEVEL BUSINESS CASE IS DEVELOPED FOR THE PROGRAM					
	1	2	3	4	5
4. I am aware of the contents of the high-level business case that was prepared for my program.					
ELEMENT 1.5 A NUMBER OF GATES OR STAGES ARE IDENTIFIED WHEN PROGRAM STATUS (INCLUDING BENEFITS REALIZATION) WILL BE REVIEWED					
	1	2	3	4	5
5. I understand why our organization uses a governance process with stage gates, and I know why the specific approach to governance was selected for my program.					
TOTAL – DEFINING					
2.0 Initiating the Program					
ELEMENT 2.1 A PROGRAM CHARTER IS PREPARED					
	1	2	3	4	5
1. I participate in the development of my program's charter and am aware of the constraints that affect my program.					
ELEMENT 2.2 THE PROGRAM VISION IS DOCUMENTED TO DESCRIBE THE END STATE AND ITS BENEFIT TO THE ORGANIZATION					
	1	2	3	4	5
2. I understand the vision for my program and how it links to my organization's ongoing work and strategic objectives.					

ELEMENT 2.3 KEY PROGRAM DECISION MAKERS ARE IDENTIFIED					
	1	2	3	4	5
3. I know the key decision makers on my program and their roles and responsibilities.					

ELEMENT 2.4 STAKEHOLDER EXPECTATIONS AND INTERESTS ARE IDENTIFIED					
	1	2	3	4	5
4. I have a list of the key stakeholders and their attitudes toward my program, which I use in preparing an initial strategy to manage and work with them.					

ELEMENT 2.5 HIGH-LEVEL RISKS TO THE PROGRAM ARE IDENTIFIED					
	1	2	3	4	5
5. I have a documented list of the high-level risks that are known at the time the program is selected.					

ELEMENT 2.6 CANDIDATE PROJECTS TO BE IN THE PROGRAM, AS WELL AS NON-PROJECT WORK, ARE IDENTIFIED					
	1	2	3	4	5
6. I know the decision-making criteria, which I will follow when projects and other work are proposed to be part of my program.					

ELEMENT 2.7 AN INITIAL INFRASTRUCTURE FOR PROGRAM MANAGEMENT IS DETERMINED					
	1	2	3	4	5
7. I understand the rationale that was used to determine the initial roadmap for my program and the needed infrastructure.					

ELEMENT 2.8 THE TIMETABLE TO COMPLETE THE PROGRAM IS DETERMINED					
	1	2	3	4	5
8. I have a high-level schedule that was prepared during program initiation that shows the time needed to complete my program.					

ELEMENT 2.9 INITIAL ESTIMATES OF THE PROGRAM'S COST ARE PREPARED					
	1	2	3	4	5
9. I understand the funding goals and structure proposed for my program and the initial cost estimate that was prepared.					

ELEMENT 2.10 KEY RESOURCES FOR PROGRAM MANAGEMENT ARE IDENTIFIED TO SET UP THE PROGRAM					
	1	2	3	4	5
10. I have a list of the proposed resources my program required for its initial stages.					

ELEMENT 2.11 THE PROGRAM CHARTER IS APPROVED

	1	2	3	4	5
11. I have received formal approval from the Program Governance Board for my program charter, which shows my own authority to apply resources to my program.					
TOTAL – INITIATING					

3.0 Planning the Program

ELEMENT 3.1 A PROGRAM MANAGEMENT PLAN IS PREPARED

	1	2	3	4	5
1. I prepare a program management plan for my program and integrate subsidiary plans into it.					

ELEMENT 3.2 A BENEFITS REALIZATION PLAN IS PREPARED

	1	2	3	4	5
2. I prepare a benefits realization plan for my program with metrics to use to track progress in benefits delivery and to show what must be done to transition my program, when it is complete, to sustain these benefits.					

ELEMENT 3.3 KEY PROGRAM RISKS AND ISSUES ARE IDENTIFIED

	1	2	3	4	5
3. I hold a risk management planning meeting and prepare a risk management plan that, among other things, shows the approach I will use to manage interdependencies between risks on the projects and non-project work on my program.					

ELEMENT 3.4 THE PROGRAM'S BUDGET IS DETERMINED

	1	2	3	4	5
4. I document the funding goals for my program and establish a budget baseline, which are part of my program's financial management plan.					

ELEMENT 3.5 DEPENDENCIES, CONSTRAINTS, AND ASSUMPTIONS ARE DOCUMENTED

	1	2	3	4	5
5. I prepare a scope statement that documents boundaries, assumptions, and constraints for my program.					

ELEMENT 3.6 A STRATEGY TO MANAGE THE PROGRAM AND ITS COMPONENTS IS AGREED UPON AND DOCUMENTED

	1	2	3	4	5
6. I document the approaches I follow to structure the various projects in my program such as an architecture baseline, a Program Work Breakdown Structure (PWBS), a procurement management plan, a contract management plan, and criteria to initiate projects and non-project work.					

ELEMENT 3.7 NECESSARY FEASIBILITY STUDIES ARE CONDUCTED

	1	2	3	4	5
7. I realize that external events will affect my program and document them and conduct benchmarking and feasibility studies as needed.					

ELEMENT 3.8 A ROADMAP OR ARCHITECTURE TO SHOWING THE INTERRELATIONSHIPS AMONG THE COMPONENT PROJECTS AND NON-PROJECT WORK IN THE PROGRAM IS PREPARED

	1	2	3	4	5
8. I use the initial program roadmap but update it to show the relationships between the projects in my programs and the non-project work and the outcomes expected.					

ELEMENT 3.9 A COMMUNICATIONS STRATEGY FOR EACH KEY STAKEHOLDER IS DETERMINED

	1	2	3	4	5
9. I establish a strategy to communicate with stakeholders on my program and prepare a stakeholder management plan, a stakeholder inventory, and a stakeholder management strategy; to assist in this process, I use a variety of approaches to identify program stakeholders.					

ELEMENT 3.10 A PROGRAM MANAGEMENT OFFICE (PMO) IS APPROVED AND IMPLEMENTED

	1	2	3	4	5
10. I obtain approval to establish a PMO for my program with a detailed charter describing its roles and responsibilities.					

ELEMENT 3.11 TOOLS, PROCESSES, AND TECHNIQUES REQUIRED FOR PROGRAM MANAGEMENT ARE OBTAINED

	1	2	3	4	5
11. I establish a Program Management Information System and use a variety of tools and techniques to support my program and my team.					

ELEMENT 3.12 THE PROGRAM MANAGEMENT PLAN IS APPROVED

	1	2	3	4	5
12. I obtain formal approval from my Program Governance Board of my program management plan.					

ELEMENT 3.13 A PROGRAM MANAGEMENT GOVERNANCE STRUCTURE IS DETERMINED

	1	2	3	4	5
13. I prepare a program governance plan that details roles and responsibilities and the approaches to follow for stage gate reviews and periodic health checks.					

ELEMENT 3.14 A PROGRAM CONTROL FRAMEWORK IS ESTABLISHED TO ASSIST IN BENEFIT MEASUREMENT AS WELL AS IN OVERALL MANAGEMENT OF THE PROGRAM'S COMPONENTS

	1	2	3	4	5
14. I use a program management methodology as I manage my program.					
TOTAL – PLANNING					

4.0 Executing the Program					

ELEMENT 4.1 PROJECTS ARE INITIATED AS PART OF THE PROGRAM

	1	2	3	4	5
1. I submit requests based on business cases to initiate projects in my program to the Governance Board and execute the program management plan.					

ELEMENT 4.2 SHARED RESOURCES NEEDED FOR COMPONENT PROJECTS AND THE NON-PROJECT WORK ARE COORDINATED

	1	2	3	4	5
2. I monitor resource use on my program and will reallocate resources as necessary to support any approved changes.					

ELEMENT 4.3 CHANGE REQUESTS ARE REVIEWED

	1	2	3	4	5
3. I establish and follow a change control system for my program.					

ELEMENT 4.4 ADDITIONAL WORK IS AUTHORIZED AS REQUIRED

	1	2	3	4	5
4. I recognize changes affecting my program may lead to the need to change the projects and non-project work and, if they are approved, I then update the program management plan.					

ELEMENT 4.5 COMMUNICATIONS WITH STAKEHOLDERS IS FOSTERED AND ENCOURAGED AT ALL LEVELS

	1	2	3	4	5
5. I follow my stakeholder management plan and actively communicate with my stakeholders and track their participation in my program.					

ELEMENT 4.6 COMMUNICATIONS WITH MEMBERS OF THE PROGRAM GOVERNANCE BOARD OCCURS ON A REGULAR BASIS

	1	2	3	4	5
6. I meet regularly with my Program Governance Board and provide information to them on a scheduled and ad hoc basis.					

ELEMENT 4.7 ALIGNMENT OF THE PROGRAM'S GOALS, AND ITS BENEFITS, IS ASSESSED AGAINST THAT OF THE ORGANIZATION

	1	2	3	4	5
7. Based on continuous use of lessons learned on my program, I provide suggestions for updates to our organization's policies, procedures, and processes.					

ELEMENT 4.8 COMMON ACTIVITIES AMONG THE PROGRAM'S PROJECTS AND NON-PROJECT WORK ARE COORDINATED

	1	2	3	4	5
8. I manage the interrelationships between the projects and non-project work in my program to coordinate common activities.					

ELEMENT 4.9 DEPENDENCIES WITH OTHER ORGANIZATIONAL INITIATIVES ARE COORDINATED

	1	2	3	4	5
9. I conduct lessons learned meetings with my team and other stakeholders, and I support our organization's knowledge management system.					

ELEMENT 4.10 THE PROGRAM MANAGEMENT PLAN IS EXECUTED

	1	2	3	4	5
10. I follow the program management plan and document the benefits that are realized and the completed deliverables.					
TOTAL – EXECUTING					

5.0 Monitoring and Controlling the Program

ELEMENT 5.1 PROGRESS IS ANALYZED ACCORDING TO THE PROGRAM MANAGEMENT PLAN

	1	2	3	4	5
1. I set up a process to make sure each of the projects in my program meets requirements, and I also monitor suppliers who support the overall program regularly.					

ELEMENT 5.2 BENEFIT REALIZATION IS ANALYZED ACCORDING TO THE BENEFITS REALIZATION PLAN					
	1	2	3	4	5
2. I prepare a benefits realization report with specific metrics to show progress to my program stakeholders and the Program Governance Board on a regular basis.					

ELEMENT 5.3 ISSUES AND RISKS ARE CONTINUOUSLY IDENTIFIED, AND CORRECTIVE ACTIONS ARE TAKEN AS REQUIRED					
	1	2	3	4	5
3. On my program, I oversee risks at the program level, determine the effectiveness of risk responses, and track program issues.					

ELEMENT 5.4 EXTERNAL ENVIRONMENTAL CHANGES ARE ANALYZED TO DETERMINE THE POSSIBLE IMPACT ON THE PROGRAM AND ITS REALIZATION OF BENEFITS					
	1	2	3	4	5
4. I identify external changes to determine their impact on my program, especially in terms of overall priority within our portfolio and in benefit delivery.					

ELEMENT 5.5 GOVERNANCE OVERSIGHT IS REGULARLY PRACTICED AT THE PROGRAM AND PROJECT LEVELS					
	1	2	3	4	5
5. I follow our established governance process, taking corrective and preventive actions as needed and recommended.					

ELEMENT 5.6 PROGRAM CHANGES ARE ANALYZED IN ACCORDANCE WITH ESTABLISHED PROCEDURES					
	1	2	3	4	5
6. I setup an integrated change control system for my program.					

ELEMENT 5.7 PROGRAM EXECUTION IS MONITORED ACCORDING TO THE PROGRAM MANAGEMENT PLAN					
	1	2	3	4	5
7. I monitor overall program execution according to the program management plan and prepare forecasts to predict the likelihood of achieving our planned outcomes.					

ELEMENT 5.8 SCHEDULE SLIPPAGES AND OPPORTUNITIES ARE IDENTIFIED AND MANAGED					
	1	2	3	4	5
8. I follow the program's schedule and use metrics for schedule control.					

ELEMENT 5.9 PROACTIVE COST CONTROL IS PRACTICED					
	1	2	3	4	5
9. I conduct financial status reviews and have a cost management system to document impacts from overruns or under-runs and any needed changes to the program management plan.					

ELEMENT 5.10 STAKEHOLDER EXPECTATIONS ARE MANAGED					
	1	2	3	4	5
10. I work actively to communicate with program stakeholders, monitor their participation, and negotiate with them to resolve conflicts as needed.					

ELEMENT 5.11 PERFORMANCE DATA ARE CONSOLIDATED TO DETERMINE APPROPRIATE RESOURCE USE TO DELIVER BENEFITS					
	1	2	3	4	5
11. I have a process to consolidate data from my projects and other work in my program, along with regular status reviews to provide my stakeholders with performance data and progress in benefits delivery.					

ELEMENT 5.12 COMPONENTS TRANSITION TO CLOSURE					
	1	2	3	4	5
12. When each project is ready for closure, I submit a formal request to the Program Governance Board.					
TOTAL – MONITORING AND CONTROLLING					

6.0 Closing the Program					

ELEMENT 6.1 THE PROGRAM IS FORMALLY CLOSED					
	1	2	3	4	5
1. I obtain formal acceptance from customers and my sponsor before closing my program.					

ELEMENT 6.2 PRODUCES AND SERVICES TRANSITION TO OPERATIONS					
	1	2	3	4	5
2. I follow the program's transition plan to transition the benefits of my program to customers, end users, or operational or customer support groups and document this acceptance.					

ELEMENT 6.3 PROGRAM BENEFITS ARE REALIZED					
	1	2	3	4	5
3. I evaluate the benefits realized by my program with those in the benefits realization plan in a benefits realization report.					

ELEMENT 6.4 CUSTOMER SUPPORT IS PROVIDED (AS APPLICABLE, SUCH AS DEFINED IN A CONTRACT)					
	1	2	3	4	5
4. I document whether the program goals were met and provide support to customers as needed, even after the program is officially closed, should questions arise.					

ELEMENT 6.5 LESSONS LEARNED ARE INTEGRATED INTO THE ORGANIZATION'S KNOWLEDGE MANAGEMENT SYSTEM					
	1	2	3	4	5
5. I publish lessons learned on my program and maintain them so they can be easily accessed by others and can be part of our organization's knowledge management system.					

ELEMENT 6.6 FEEDBACK IS PROVIDED ON AREAS OUTSIDE THE SCOPE OF THE PROGRAM					
	1	2	3	4	5
6. I analyze the results and lessons learned from my program to see if there are impacts that can affect other parts of our organization.					

ELEMENT 6.7 PROGRAM DOCUMENTS ARE ARCHIVED FOR FUTURE REUSE					
	1	2	3	4	5
7. I prepare a final program report and make sure all program documents are archived following our organization's archive plan.					

ELEMENT 6.8 CONTRACTUAL OBLIGATIONS ARE MET					
	1	2	3	4	5
8. I review program contracts to make sure deliverables and sign-offs are complete, and I conduct a review of supplier performance and document results in a procurement report.					

ELEMENT 6.9 INTELLECTUAL PROPERTY IS CAPTURED FOR REUSE					
	1	2	3	4	5
9. I release team resources after making sure intellectual property from my program is captured for reuse.					

ELEMENT 6.10 A LEGACY OF BENEFIT SUSTAINMENT IS ACHIEVED					
	1	2	3	4	5
10. I verify that my program has added value and that its benefits will be sustained.					
TOTAL – CLOSING					
TOTAL – ALL PERFORMANCE COMPETENCIES					

These questions involve the personal competencies.

1.0 Communicating					
ELEMENT: 1.1 ACTIVELY LISTENS, UNDERSTANDS, AND RESPONDS TO STAKEHOLDERS					
	1	2	3	4	5
1. I practice a policy of active listening and being present and attentive each time I communicate with my program stakeholders.					
ELEMENT 1.2 USES THE KEY CHANNELS OF COMMUNICATIONS					
	1	2	3	4	5
2. I follow our established information distribution process and use both formal and informal methods when communicating with my stakeholders.					
ELEMENT 1.3 ENSURES THE QUALITY OF THE INFORMATION THAT IS COMMUNICATED					
	1	2	3	4	5
3. I provide information that is accurate and factual as I provide consistent messages to my stakeholders.					
ELEMENT 1.4 TAILORS THE INFORMATION TO THE AUDIENCE					
	1	2	3	4	5
4. I recognize that different stakeholders require different types of communications and work to use each stakeholder's preferred communication's approach as I work with my program stakeholders.					
ELEMENT 1.5 EFFECTIVELY USES EACH OF THE DIFFERENT COMMUNICATIONS DIMENSIONS					
	1	2	3	4	5
5. I use different communications skills as I interact with my program stakeholders and work to overcome my own barriers or difficulties in communicating.					
TOTAL – COMMUNICATING					

2.0 Unit of Competence: Leading					
ELEMENT 2.1 IMPLEMENTS THE PROGRAM'S VISION					
	1	2	3	4	5
1. I regularly discuss the vision of my program in meetings with my team and other stakeholders to ensure there is mutual understanding of its importance.					
ELEMENT 2.2 ESTABLISHES THE PROGRAM'S DIRECTION					
	1	2	3	4	5
2. To clarify perceptions of the program, I document and discuss its critical success factors and describe the importance of the program to my stakeholders.					

ELEMENT 2.3 RECOGNIZES THE INTERDEPENDENCIES WITHIN THE PROGRAM

	1	2	3	4	5
3. I document the interdependencies between projects within my program, and I review proposed business cases for new projects and the need to terminate others that no longer support the program or are complete.					

ELEMENT 2.4 TAKES CALCULATED RISKS; IS VENTURESOME

	1	2	3	4	5
4. I know when I should take a risk and am willing to try new ideas even if others object.					

ELEMENT 2.5 ASSUMES OWNERSHIP FOR THE PROGRAM

	1	2	3	4	5
5. I demonstrate ownership for the program through my active involvement in it and my own alignment of my personal priorities to that of the program.					
TOTAL – LEADING					

3.0 Unit of Competence: Building Relationships

ELEMENT 3.1 BUILDS TRUST AMONG STAKEHOLDERS, CLIENTS, AND TEAM MEMBERS

	1	2	3	4	5
1. I realize the importance of demonstrating a genuine interest in my stakeholder's concerns and confide in them to promote a "win-win" attitude.					

ELEMENT 3.2 LEVERAGES THE ORGANIZATION'S POLITICAL DYNAMICS TO PROMOTE PROGRAM GOALS

	1	2	3	4	5
2. I work to garner support among the key stakeholders, recognizing the internal dynamics affecting my program and establish a network of trusted sources to assist me in program management.					

ELEMENT 3.3 ADVOCATES FOR DIVERSITY AND TREATS OTHERS WITH COURTESY AND RESPECT

	1	2	3	4	5
3. I strive to establish a diverse program team, treating each team member with courtesy and respect so people will express points of view openly and freely.					

ELEMENT 3.4 ESTABLISHES AND DEMONSTRATES HIGH STANDARDS FOR PERSONAL AND TEAM MEMBER PERFORMANCE

	1	2	3	4	5
4. I document each team member's individual performance plan to make sure it supports the overall program goals and objectives, and I meet regularly with my team members to review performance and assess progress.					

ELEMENT 3.5 PROMOTES AND DEMONSTRATES ETHICS, INTEGRITY, AND ADHERENCE TO CORPORATE VALUES IN ALL INTERACTIONS					
	1	2	3	4	5
5. I ask each team member to sign an ethics or conflict-of-interest statement and establish a policy to enforce the ethics code on my program.					
TOTAL – BUILDING RELATIONSHIPS					

4.0 Unit of Competence: Negotiating

ELEMENT 4.1 OBTAINS NEEDED PROGRAM RESOURCES					
	1	2	3	4	5
1. I actively work to obtain needed resources for my program by explaining its importance and keeping my team apprised of my progress.					

ELEMENT 4.2 ENSURES PROGRAM ALIGNMENT WITH THE ORGANIZATION'S STRATEGIES					
	1	2	3	4	5
2. I regularly communicate with strategic planners and members of the portfolio review board to ensure my program remains in alignment with organizational priorities as I seek opportunities to enhance its value to the organization.					

ELEMENT 4.3 WORKS PROACTIVELY WITH THE PROGRAM GOVERNANCE BOARD					
	1	2	3	4	5
3. I seek ideas and feedback from members of the Program Governance Board regularly, not solely at stage gate reviews or health checks, to obtain suggestions on ways to improve overall program performance.					

ELEMENT 4.4 PROMOTES OVERALL STAKEHOLDER SUPPORT					
	1	2	3	4	5
4. I use a variety of negotiating techniques as I work with different stakeholder groups to obtain support for my program, and I reach out to stakeholders to resolve issues of concern.					
TOTAL – NEGOTIATING					

5.0 Unit of Competence: Thinking Critically

ELEMENT 5.1 CONDUCTS ONGOING ANALYSES TO IDENTIFY TRENDS, VARIANCES, AND ISSUES					
	1	2	3	4	5
1. I assess the program's environment to help identify trends, variances, and issues in a proactive manner, and I monitor stakeholder attitudes and perceptions to avoid any negative influences.					

ELEMENT 5.2 APPLIES FACT-BASED DECISION MAKING TO CURRENT AND PROSPECTIVE ISSUES					
	1	2	3	4	5
2. I make decisions as much as possible based on facts and review them, if time permits, with my stakeholders to discuss any alternatives to consider.					

ELEMENT 5.3 WORKS PROACTIVELY WITH THE PROGRAM GOVERNANCE STRUCTURE THAT PROVIDES FOR DECISION MAKING AT THE APPROPRIATE LEVELS					
	1	2	3	4	5
3. I delegate decisions as much as possible to my team but recognize when decisions and issues should be elevated to the Program Governance Board for resolution.					

ELEMENT 5.4 CONSTRUCTIVELY CHALLENGES COMMON BELIEFS AND ASSUMPTIONS—ALWAYS LOOKING FOR A BETTER WAY					
	1	2	3	4	5
4. I encourage innovation and creativity as I solve problems, and I reach out to stakeholders for their ideas even if in the process I need to challenge current practices, assumptions, and constraints.					
TOTAL – THINKING CRITICALLY					

6.0 Unit of Competence: Facilitating					

ELEMENT 6.1 PLANS FOR SUCCESS FROM THE START OF THE PROGRAM					
	1	2	3	4	5
1. I follow an approach in which we build on early successes in our program to foster a team attitude that realizes later successes will result.					

ELEMENT 6.2 ENSURES THAT ALL TEAM MEMBERS WORK TOGETHER TO ACHIEVE PROGRAM GOALS					
	1	2	3	4	5
2. I conduct kick-off meetings and work to get my team members to quickly cooperate, collaborate, and support one another.					

ELEMENT 6.3 EFFECTIVELY RESOLVES ISSUES TO SOLVE PROBLEMS					
	1	2	3	4	5
3. I strive to resolve issues by observing trends, discrepancies, and unexpected changes, and I use and track issue and action-item logs to ensure problems raised are solved.					

ELEMENT 6.4 EFFECTIVELY HANDLES PERSONAL AND TEAM ADVERSITY

	1	2	3	4	5
4. I work to resolve problems objectively and take responsibility if there are failures or the need to make revisions to our plans and processes as I practice a policy of learning from mistakes.					
TOTAL – FACILITATING					

7.0 Unit of Competence: Mentoring

ELEMENT 7.1 SUPPORTS MENTORING FOR PROGRAM TEAM MEMBERS

	1	2	3	4	5
1. I work to maintain a motivated team and show a personal interest in the development of my team members.					

ELEMENT 7.2 ESTABLISHES A FORMAL MENTORING PROGRAM

	1	2	3	4	5
2. I provide opportunities for my team members to participate in mentoring programs if desired, and I serve as an informal mentor offering suggestions in a casual and indirect way.					

ELEMENT 7.3 SUPPORTS INDIVIDUAL AND TEAM DEVELOPMENT ACTIVITIES

	1	2	3	4	5
3. I provide suggestions to my team regarding the organization's career path in program management, and I provide information on possible individual and team development opportunities.					

ELEMENT 7.4 RECOGNIZES AND REWARDS INDIVIDUAL AND TEAM ACCOMPLISHMENTS

	1	2	3	4	5
4. I work to celebrate success with my team when there are team accomplishments, and I recognize key people when there are individual accomplishments.					
TOTAL – MENTORING					

8.0 Unit of Competence: Embracing Changes

ELEMENT 8.1 ESTABLISHES AN ENVIRONMENT RECEPTIVE TO CHANGE

	1	2	3	4	5
1. I promote an atmosphere that is receptive to change by meeting regularly with stakeholders and discussing feedback received with my team.					

ELEMENT 8.2 INFLUENCES FACTORS THAT MAY RESULT IN CHANGE					
	1	2	3	4	5
2. I work proactively with stakeholders to identify factors in advance that may require a change and provide feedback to my team.					
ELEMENT 8.3 PLANS FOR CHANGE AND ITS POTENTIAL IMPACT					
	1	2	3	4	5
3. I strive to adapt to environmental changes to minimize any adverse impacts on my program.					
ELEMENT 8.4 MANAGES CHANGES WHEN THEY DO OCCUR					
	1	2	3	4	5
4. I demonstrate a flexible approach and attitude when a change does affect my program so it is viewed in a positive manner by my team members and other stakeholders.					
TOTAL: EMBRACING CHANGES					
TOTAL: ALL PERSONAL COMPETENCIES					

Appendix C: Use by Prospective Program Managers

As more and more organizations turn toward program management, there is a need for more people who are interested in being program managers. Building on the competency model, in the performance and personal competencies, people can use the following questionnaire to evaluate their readiness in becoming a program manager or to see if additional training or mentoring may be required in certain areas.

This questionnaire differs in that it is set up in a multiple choice format to test one's knowledge as to what a program manager should do in each of the elements in the model.

1.0 Defining the Program			

ELEMENT: 1.1 STRATEGIC BENEFITS OF THE PROGRAM ARE UNDERSTOOD BY ALL STAKEHOLDERS

	A	B	C	D
1. Before a program is submitted for possible selection, it is important to analyze the expected benefits of program stakeholders in a:	Benefits statement	Strategic directive	Stakeholder log	Prioritized list

ELEMENT 1.2 A PLAN TO INITIATE THE PROGRAM IS PREPARED

	A	B	C	D
2. The document that describes how the program will be initiated is the:	Project charter	Business case	High-level plan	Program brief

ELEMENT 1.3 THE PROGRAM'S OBJECTIVES ARE ALIGNED WITH THE STRATEGIC GOALS OF THE ORGANIZATION

	A	B	C	D
3. One criterion to consider when determining whether or not to select a program is to assess its:	Deliverables	Results	Objectives	Values

ELEMENT 1.4 A HIGH-LEVEL BUSINESS CASE IS DEVELOPED FOR THE PROGRAM

	A	B	C	D
4. To document the needs, benefits, feasibility, and justification for a program, one should prepare a:	Business case	Strategic directive	Mission statement	Program vision

ELEMENT 1.5 A NUMBER OF GATES OR STAGES ARE IDENTIFIED WHEN PROGRAM STATUS (INCLUDING BENEFIT REALIZATION) WILL BE REVIEWED

	A	B	C	D
5. In order to determine whether or not a program is on track, one should use:	Milestones	Gates	Portfolio management	Forecasts

TOTAL – DEFINING

2.0 Initiating the Program			

ELEMENT 2.1 A PROGRAM CHARTER IS PREPARED

	A	B	C	D
1. The document, when approved, that is used to move to the Program Set Up phase is the:	Business case	High-level plan	Program roadmap	Program charter

ELEMENT 2.2 THE PROGRAM VISION IS DOCUMENTED TO SHOW THE END STATE AND ITS BENEFIT TO THE ORGANIZATION

	A	B	C	D
2. The end state of the program is its:	Vision	Mission	Deliverables	Results

ELEMENT 2.3 KEY PROGRAM DECISION MAKERS ARE IDENTIFIED

	A	B	C	D
3. The executive sponsor and the program manager are appointed during which phase in the program management life cycle?	Pre-program preparations	Program initiation	Program set up	Defining

ELEMENT 2.4 STAKEHOLDER EXPECTATIONS AND INTERESTS ARE IDENTIFIED

	A	B	C	D
4. The link between business strategy and planned or unplanned work is part of the:	Business case	Charter	Roadmap	High-level plan

ELEMENT 2.5 HIGH-LEVEL RISKS TO THE PROGRAM ARE IDENTIFIED

	A	B	C	D
5. One approach to consider in identifying high-level risks is use of a:	Probability matrix	Decision tree	Sensitivity analysis	SWOT analysis

ELEMENT 2.6 CANDIDATE PROJECTS TO BE IN THE PROGRAM, AS WELL AS NON-PROJECT WORK, ARE IDENTIFIED

	A	B	C	D
6. The document that shows how components are organized by stages or blocks is the:	Architecture	Roadmap	Prioritized list	Business case

ELEMENT 2.7 AN INITIAL INFRASTRUCTURE FOR PROGRAM MANAGEMENT IS DETERMINED

	A	B	C	D
7. A high-level snapshot of the program's infrastructure is contained in the:	Program charter	Business case	PMO charter	Roadmap

ELEMENT 2.8 THE TIMETABLE TO COMPLETE THE PROGRAM IS DETERMINED

	A	B	C	D
8. An order-of-magnitude schedule is prepared during which of the following phases in the program management life cycle?	Program initiation	Pre-program preparations	Program set up	Initiate program

ELEMENT 2.9 INITIAL ESTIMATES OF THE PROGRAM'S COST ARE PREPARED

	A	B	C	D
9. An initial cost estimate is contained in the program's:	Governance plan	Financial framework	Cost management plan	Project charter

ELEMENT 2.10 KEY RESOURCES FOR PROGRAM MANAGEMENT ARE IDENTIFIED TO SET UP THE PROGRAM

	A	B	C	D
10. For the initial stages of the program, you should prepare a list of required resources. This is done by preparing a (an):	Budget estimate	Resource plan	Order-of-magnitude estimate	Resource baseline

ELEMENT 2.11 THE PROGRAM CHARTER IS APPROVED

	A	B	C	D
11. The program charter is approved and signed off by:	The sponsor	The executive director	The program manager	The Program Governance Board

TOTAL – INITIATING

3.0 Planning the Program

ELEMENT 3.1 A PROGRAM MANAGEMENT PLAN IS PREPARED

	A	B	C	D
1. The key elements of program direction and management are contained in the:	Program management plan	Program execution plan	Program manager's charter	Program roadmap

ELEMENT 3.2 A BENEFITS REALIZATION PLAN IS PREPARED

	A	B	C	D
2. Metrics to use to track progress in benefits delivery are contained in the:	Program performance reports	Benefits realization plan	Benefits realization report	Program requirements document

ELEMENT 3.3 KEY PROGRAM RISKS AND ISSUES ARE IDENTIFIED

	A	B	C	D
3. One approach to follow to identify key program risks is to:	Define risk profiles	Discuss risks at each meeting of your Program Governance Board	Determine risk tolerances	Hold a risk planning meeting

ELEMENT 3.4 THE PROGRAM'S BUDGET IS DETERMINED

	A	B	C	D
4. Analyzing your program's operational costs is useful in:	Preparing the program's financial plan	Determining the funding goals	Preparing the financial framework	Documenting a payment schedule

ELEMENT 3.5 DEPENDENCIES, CONSTRAINTS, AND ASSUMPTIONS ARE DOCUMENTED

	A	B	C	D
5. Program assumptions and constraints are documented in the program's:	Requirements document	Scope management plan	Scope statement	PWBS dictionary

ELEMENT 3.6 A STRATEGY TO MANAGE THE PROGRAM AND ITS COMPONENTS IS AGREED UPON AND DOCUMENTED

	A	B	C	D
6. One approach to foster control and communications with those in a program who are managing projects and non-project work is to prepare a:	Program vision	Program charter	PWBS	Statement of objectives

ELEMENT 3.7 NECESSARY FEASIBILITY STUDIES ARE CONDUCTED

	A	B	C	D
7. One reason it is necessary to assess market environmental factors is that they may:	Affect the change management plan	Lead to changes not documented in the business case	Require review of the charter	Change the program manager's responsibilities

ELEMENT 3.8 A ROADMAP OR ARCHITECTURE TO SHOW THE INTERRELATIONSHIPS AMONG THE COMPONENT PROJECTS AND NON-PROJECT WORK IN THE PROGRAM IS PREPARED

	A	B	C	D
8. As new projects become part of the program, you should, among other things:	Document the program's vision	Document the program's values	Baseline the architecture	Update the roadmap

ELEMENT 3.9 A COMMUNICATIONS STRATEGY FOR EACH STAKEHOLDER IS DETERMINED

	A	B	C	D
9. The scope statement, among other things, shows stakeholder acceptance criteria, but stakeholders should:	Participate in developing the stakeholder management plan	Sign off on deliverables and benefits	Receive a copy of the stakeholder management strategy	Receive updates when the register changes

ELEMENT 3.10 A PROGRAM MANAGEMENT OFFICE (PMO) IS APPROVED AND IMPLEMENTED				
	A	B	C	D
10. Program management elements and artifacts to use should be included in the:	PWBS	Scope statement	Program charter	Requirements document

ELEMENT 3.11 TOOLS, PROCESSES, AND TECHNIQUES REQUIRED FOR PROGRAM MANAGEMENT ARE OBTAINED				
	A	B	C	D
11. One approach to manage program data and information is to:	Prepare a program reporting plan	Use the same status reports for all stakeholders	Use the EPMO	Establish a PMIS

ELEMENT 3.12 THE PROGRAM MANAGEMENT PLAN IS APPROVED				
	A	B	C	D
12. The program management plan must be approved before moving to which phase in the program life cycle?	Executing	Program set up	Delivery of program benefits	Set up the program and technical infrastructure

ELEMENT 3.13 A PROGRAM MANAGEMENT GOVERNANCE STRUCTURE IS DETERMINED				
	A	B	C	D
13. Key governance roles and responsibilities are included in the:	Program architecture	Governance plan	PMO charter	Program roadmap

ELEMENT 3.14 A PROGRAM CONTROL FRAMEWORK IS ESTABLISHED TO ASSIST IN BENEFIT MEASUREMENT AS WELL AS IN OVERALL MANAGEMENT OF THE PROGRAM'S COMPONENTS				
	A	B	C	D
14. The basis for future program decisions is one purpose of the:	Scope statement	Performance plan	Business case	Program charter

TOTAL – PLANNING

4.0 Executing the Program

ELEMENT 4.1 PROJECTS ARE INITIATED AS PART OF THE PROGRAM				
	A	B	C	D
1. In order to initiate a new project for my program, I should first:	Prepare a project charter	Contact my sponsor	Prepare a business case	Meet with the Program Governance Board

ELEMENT 4.2 SHARED RESOURCES REQUIRED FOR COMPONENT PROJECTS THE NON-PROJECT WORK ARE COORDINATED				
	A	B	C	D
2. One important use of the PMIS is to:	Identify resource issues early	Show the changes required	Prepare a resource plan	Validate time reporting

ELEMENT 4.3 CHANGE REQUESTS ARE REVIEWED

	A	B	C	D
3. When one project on my program has a change, I then need to, as the program manager:	Authorize it	Determine its impact on other parts of the program	Convene a meeting of the Change Control Board (CCB)	Meet with the Program Governance Board

ELEMENT 4.4 ADDITIONAL WORK IS AUTHORIZED AS REQUIRED

	A	B	C	D
4. Assume there is a change on my program, as part of the decision-making structure that is set up, as the program manager, I should then:	Immediately recognize changes in priorities	Update the program charter	Know when to escalate it to the Program Governance Board	Update all of my plans

ELEMENT 4.5 COMMUNICATIONS WITH STAKEHOLDERS IS FOSTERED AND ENCOURAGED AT ALL LEVELS

	A	B	C3	D
5. Metrics to show stakeholder engagement activities are included in the stakeholder:	Inventory	Management strategy	Register	Management plan

ELEMENT 4.6 COMMUNICATIONS WITH MEMBERS OF THE PROGRAM GOVERNANCE BOARD OCCURS ON A REGULAR BASIS

	A	B	C	D
6. Often, during meetings with members of my Program Governance Board, I provide them with:	An update of the budget baseline	The stakeholder register	The communications log	The team's RACI or RAM chart

ELEMENT 4.7 ALIGNMENT OF THE PROGRAM'S GOALS, AND ITS BENEFITS, IS ASSESSED AGAINST THAT OF THE ORGANIZATION

	A	B	C	D
7. Because organizational priorities may change during the life of a program, I tend to document and update, when needed:	Minutes from Program Governance Board meetings	Links from each project to the organization's strategic goals	Ad hoc communications with stakeholders	Results from health checks and maturity assessments

ELEMENT 4.8 COMMON ACTIVITIES OF THE PROGRAM'S PROJECTS AND NON-PROJECT WORK ARE COORDINATED

	A	B	C	D
8. One way I make sure that common activities of the components of my program are coordinated is to:	Document minutes from meetings with components	Use the PMO	Suggest updates to corporate policies	Follow the communications management plan

ELEMENT 4.9 DEPENDENCIES WITH OTHER ORGANIZATIONAL INITIATIVES ARE COORDINATED

	A	B	C	D
9. I conduct lessons learned meetings, and also I:	Establish an organizational knowledge management system	Maintain a lessons learned database	Establish a benefits management system	Update specific project plans that are part of the program

ELEMENT 4.10 THE PROGRAM MANAGEMENT PLAN IS EXECUTED

	A	B	C	D
10. You want to show your program's benefits have been delivered so you should:	Rebaseline your benefits realization plan	Update your reports	Update your communications management plan	Document completion of your deliverables

TOTAL – EXECUTING

5.0 Monitoring and Controlling the Program

ELEMENT 5.1 PROGRESS IS ANALYZED ACCORDING TO THE PROGRAM MANAGEMENT PLAN

	A	B	C	D
1. Assume you are using a number of suppliers on your program. You then need to analyze their performance and you can do so by:	Conducting supplier reviews	Using suppliers that are on the organization's qualified seller list	Including suppliers in meetings with your team	Establishing partnering agreements from the beginning to minimize possible claims or disputes

ELEMENT 5.2 BENEFIT REALIZATION IS ANALYZED ACCORDING TO THE BENEFITS REALIZATION PLAN

	A	B	C	D
2. Benefits realization analysis is a tool and technique that is used to:	Determine if the life-cycle costs will exceed the benefits to be realized	Ensure the program delivers the promised benefits and that they translate into value	Assess the value of the benefits realization report based on a survey of stakeholders	Conduct an effective benefits review

ELEMENT 5.3 ISSUES AND RISKS ARE CONTINUOUSLY IDENTIFIED, AND CORRECTIVE ACTIONS ARE TAKEN AS REQUIRED				
	A	B	C	D
3. One way I provide oversight of risks on my program is to:	Continually identify risks at the project and program levels	Regularly update each project's risk management plan	Set up trigger conditions for risks at the program and individual project levels	Use risk audits

ELEMENT 5.4 EXTERNAL ENVIRONMENTAL CHANGES ARE ANALYZED TO DETERMINE THE POSSIBLE IMPACT ON THE PROGRAM AND ITS REALIZATION OF BENEFITS				
	A	B	C	D
4. Assume you are managing a complex program. It has the possibility of a class action lawsuit. This means you should:	Have a member from your legal department on your core team	Monitor legal issues	Ensure you have continual governance oversight	Set up an issue resolution process and follow it throughout your program

ELEMENT 5.5 GOVERNANCE OVERSIGHT IS REGULARLY PRACTICED AT THE PROGRAM AND PROJECT LEVELS				
	A	B	C	D
5. One way I make sure I am following suggestions from my Program Governance Board is that I use a:	Governance decision register	Governance tracking log	Governance report	Governance performance plan

ELEMENT 5.6 PROGRAM CHANGES ARE IMPLEMENTED IN ACCORDANCE WITH ESTABLISHED INTEGRATED CHANGE CONTROL PROCEDURES				
	A	B	C	D
6. A best practice that I would follow on my program is to first use:	A change request form for each proposed change	A change request log	An integrated change control process	A meeting of the Change Control Board (CCB)

ELEMENT 5.7 PROGRAM EXECUTION IS MONITORED ACCORDING TO THE PROGRAM MANAGEMENT PLAN				
	A	B	C	D
7. One approach I would use on a program to predict the likelihood of achieving my planned outcomes is:	Trend analysis	Regular status reporting	Earned value	PMIS

ELEMENT 5.8 SCHEDULE SLIPPAGES AND OPPORTUNITIES ARE IDENTIFIED AND MANAGED

	A	B	C	D
8. We tend to focus our emphasis in schedule control on ways in which we can make up any delays that have occurred on our programs. But attention also is needed on documenting:	Preventive actions	Minutes from supplier reviews	Opportunities to accelerate the schedule	The Complete Performance Index

ELEMENT 5.9 PROACTIVE COST CONTROL IS FOLLOWED

	A	B	C	D
9. In analyzing the work of suppliers on a program, a best practice to follow for potential cost impact is to:	Establish a budget management system	Conduct a variance analysis	Conduct lessons learned sessions	Use benchmarking data

ELEMENT 5.10 STAKEHOLDER EXPECTATIONS ARE MANAGED

	A	B	C	D
10. Assume you have over 100 different stakeholders on your program and have set up 12 stakeholder groups for effective management. You want to make sure all stakeholders participate, so you should:	Set up leads for each of the groups and meet with them one-on-one weekly or biweekly	Use a stakeholder communications log	Survey each stakeholder monthly for ideas	Make sure all stakeholders receive the same information regardless of whether they are internal or external

ELEMENT 5.11 PERFORMANCE DATA ARE CONSOLIDATED TO DETERMINE APPROPRIATE RESOURCE USE TO DELIVER BENEFITS

	A	B	C	D
11. On my program, each time I hold a status review meeting, I:	Communicate the results to all my stakeholders	Notify all my stakeholders in advance so they can attend even if they do so virtually	Document minutes and action items	Ensure that each person who attends has an opportunity to speak

ELEMENT 5.12 COMPONENTS TRANSITION TO CLOSURE

	A	B	C	D
12. Before closing a project on my program, I:	Evaluate team member performance	Reallocate resources to other projects or other parts of the organization	Dismantle the PMO	Document a request to close the project and present it to the Program Governance Board

TOTAL– MONITORING AND CONTROLLING

6.0 Closing the Program

ELEMENT 6.1 THE PROGRAM IS FORMALLY CLOSED

	A	B	C	D
1. In closing my program, it is necessary to close its financial activities. As a program manager, a major activity to perform is to:	Conduct a final earned value analysis	Finalize the budget baseline	Meet with the financial department to discuss lessons learned	Provide a full-scope verification audit and accounting of financial records

ELEMENT 6.2 PRODUCTS AND SERVICES TRANSITION TO OPERATIONS

	A	B	C	D
2. Before my program can transition to operations, it is important to ensure that:	Documented acceptance from operations is obtained	The same core team will work with operations	The program has met all business case deliverables	The benefits realization report is finalized

ELEMENT 6.3 PROGRAM BENEFITS ARE REALIZED

	A	B	C	D
3. One way to ensure that all the benefits in the program have been realized is to:	Compare the realized benefits with those stated during the benefits identification stage of the benefits life cycle	Meet with stakeholders to discuss any outstanding issues	Evaluate the realized benefits with those listed in the business case	Receive formal approval from all Program Governance Board members

ELEMENT 6.4 CUSTOMER SUPPORT IS PROVIDED (AS APPLICABLE, SUCH AS DEFINED IN A CONTRACT)				
	A	B	C	D
4. Assume your program was handled through a contract. Future maintenance support is:	Handled as an additional procurement	Contained in the RFP	Detailed in the contract	Provided as discussed and documented with your customer

ELEMENT 6.5 LESSONS LEARNED ARE INTEGRATED INTO THE ORGANIZATION'S KNOWLEDGE MANAGEMENT SYSTEM				
	A	B	C	D
5. On my program, I publish lessons learned and incorporate them into the:	Final report	Knowledge management system	Final review with the sponsor	Final review with the team

ELEMENT 6.6 FEEDBACK IS PROVIDED ON AREAS OUTSIDE THE SCOPE OF THE PROGRAM				
	A	B	C	D
6. On my program, one of my team members discussed a lesson learned, but it did not affect our program. I then:	Placed it in the knowledge repository for this program for future reference	Suggested the team member consider it on the next program or project	Provided it to our Enterprise Program Management Office (EPMO) to pass on to other programs and projects	Discussed it with our program stakeholders

ELEMENT 6.7 PROGRAM DOCUMENTS ARE ARCHIVED FOR FUTURE REUSE				
	A	B	C	D
7. In closing the program, I have asked my core team to archive program documents. They should, as a best practice:	Place them in the knowledge repository	Set up a discussion forum to discuss them before formal closure	Survey the entire team for areas of future improvement	Index them

ELEMENT 6.8 CONTRACTUAL OBLIGATIONS ARE MET				
	A	B	C	D
8. In finalizing the procurement aspects of my program, it is important to:	Conduct an audit of each contract	Document sign-offs by our organization and the supplier	Include all aspects of the contract in the final archives	Document preventive actions

ELEMENT 6.9 INTELLECTUAL PROPERTY IS CAPTURED FOR REUSE				
	A	B	C	D
9. It is critical to reuse intellectual property gained on the program. But, in doing so, as a program manager:	Confidentiality agreements should be followed	Interviews should be held with standard questions with all team members before they leave the team	Emphasize that the intellectual property only remain with the team itself	Interface actively with the Knowledge Management Office
ELEMENT 6.10 A LEGACY OF BENEFIT SUSTAINMENT IS ACHIEVED				
	A	B	C	D
10. At the end of each program, as the program manager, it is important to make sure the products and services of the program add value. This can best be done by:	Documenting user experience	Verifying support for the new product or service	Surveying the program's stakeholders	Setting up a new life cycle to focus more on benefit sustainment
TOTAL – CLOSING				
TOTAL – ALL PERFORMANCE COMPETENCIES				

These questions involve personal competencies.

1.0 Communicating				
ELEMENT: 1.1 ACTIVELY LISTENS, UNDERSTANDS, AND RESPONDS TO STAKEHOLDERS				
	A	B	C	D
1. If I find that I am not paying as much close attention as I should to some of the stakeholders when I am talking with them, I should:	Make sure communications are reciprocal and are not one-sided	Track each message	Use a communications log	Request that the speaker repeat the information if I do not clearly understand it
ELEMENT 1.2 USES THE KEY CHANNELS OF COMMUNICATIONS				
	A	B	C	D
2. Both informal and formal communications are useful. Informal communications are preferred for:	Day-to-day activities	Results from meetings	Overall program status	Surveys
ELEMENT 1.3 ENSURES THE QUALITY OF THE INFORMATION THAT IS COMMUNICATED				
	A	B	C	D
3. Program information should be accurate and factual. At times, however, it should be validated by:	Program Governance Board members	Experts	Use of the Delphi Technique	Team members
ELEMENT 1.4 TAILORS THE INFORMATION TO THE AUDIENCE				
	A	B	C	D
4. As a program manager, it is important to determine the most suitable approach to communicate with each stakeholder group. To do so, you should:	Use the stakeholder inventory	Follow the program's information distribution process	Use the stakeholder analysis	Use the stakeholder register
ELEMENT 1.5 EFFECTIVELY USES EACH OF THE COMMUNICATIONS DIMENSIONS				
	A	B	C	D
5. Assume you are meeting with your team. To make sure everyone speaks up, one approach to use is to:	Discuss each topic and have everyone make a comment on it even if it is a repeat	Use "I" messages	Explain in advance that everyone is expected to actively participate	Ask open-ended questions
TOTAL – COMMUNICATING				

2.0 Unit of Competence: Leading			

ELEMENT 2.1 IMPLEMENTS THE PROGRAM'S VISION

	A	B	C	D
1. To describe the vision of the program to my team, I:	Refer them to the program charter	Hold a kick-off meeting	Provide each team member with a copy of it	Talk with each team member one-on-one to discuss it

ELEMENT 2.2 ESTABLISHES THE PROGRAM'S DIRECTION

	A	B	C	D
2. One way to determine the program's critical success factors is to:	Review the business case	Ask the program sponsor and other stakeholders	Use a Delphi Technique	Use the program roadmap

ELEMENT 2.3 RECOGNIZES THE INTERDEPENDENCIES WITHIN THE PROGRAM

	A	B	C	D
3. One approach to determine how the projects and the non-project work in the programs interface is to:	Prepare a component analysis	Review each of the project plans in depth	Conduct a comparative advantage analysis	Conduct a feasibility study

ELEMENT 2.4 TAKES CALCULATED RISKS; IS VENTURESOME

	A	B	C	D
4. You have decided to take risks on new ideas that seem promising. One approach to follow is to:	Conduct a risk vs. opportunity analysis meeting with your team	Use corrective action	Use preventive actions	Use focus groups

ELEMENT 2.5 ASSUMES OWNERSHIP FOR THE PROGRAM

	A	B	C	D
5. As the program manager, you are responsible for the program's success. One way to demonstrate your ownership of the program is:	Active involvement with stakeholders, especially those external to the program	Maintaining a priority list of action items	Including project managers in meetings with the Program Governance Board at key stage gates	Active involvement with stakeholders, especially members of the Program Governance Board

TOTAL – LEADING				

3.0 Unit of Competence: Building Relationships			

ELEMENT 3.1 BUILDS TRUST AMONG STAKEHOLDERS, CLIENTS, AND TEAM MEMBERS

	A	B	C	D
1. You realize that some stakeholders will be more actively involved in the program while others may only have a peripheral interest in it. You should assess:	Their opinions about the program	Their ability to influence or impact the program	The types or groups of stakeholders who will be involved to some degree	Which team member is best suited to work individually to ensure that the stakeholder's expectations are met

ELEMENT 3.2 LEVERAGES THE ORGANIZATION'S POLITICAL DYNAMICS TO PROMOTE PROGRAM GOALS

	A	B	C	D
2. You realize the importance of recognizing the internal dynamics of your organization. This means you should:	Review organizational charts and note key interfaces with the EPMO	Determine mitigation approaches to outline steps to take to manage the impact of the program on stakeholders	Review external environmental factors that may affect the program	Assess information as to likely stakeholder responses to the actions you take as program manager

ELEMENT 3.3 ADVOCATES FOR DIVERSITY AND TREATS OTHERS WITH COURTESY AND RESPECT

	A	B	C	D
3. Your goal is to have a diverse program team. Therefore, you should:	Use the organization's knowledge, skills, and competency profiles	Make sure that everyone on the team is motivated the same way, regardless of their different backgrounds	Establish a team that consists of people with different backgrounds and points of view	Prepare an Equal Opportunity Employment Plan

ELEMENT 3.4 ESTABLISHES AND DEMONSTRATES HIGH STANDARDS FOR PERSONAL AND TEAM MEMBER PERFORMANCE

	A	B	C	D
4. I realize as a program manager the importance of setting up individual performance goals and standards. A best practice to follow is to:	Evaluate performance using a 360-degree approach	Link these individual goals to the overall program goals and objectives	Make sure each of my team member's personal goals are congruent with my own personal goals	Prepare an individual development plan and provide it to each team member

ELEMENT 3.5 PROMOTES AND DEMONSTRATES ETHICS, INTEGRITY, AND ADHERENCE TO CORPORATE VALUES IN ALL INTERACTIONS

	A	B	C	D
5. Assume that on your team you want to make sure everyone understands his or her ethical responsibilities. You should:	Have each team member sign an ethics or conflict-of-interest statement	Enforce your ethics code	Make the ethics code a part of each team member's performance plan and evaluate performance against it	Prepare an ethics plan as your first step
TOTAL – BUILDING RELATIONSHIPS				

4.0 Unit of Competence: Negotiating			

ELEMENT 4.1 OBTAINS NEEDED PROGRAM RESOURCES

	A	B	C	D
1. Most program managers must obtain resources from functional managers. For effectiveness in this area, a best practice to follow is to:	Prepare a staffing management plan for your program and ask for comments from the functional managers	Use subject matter experts as you negotiate for resources with the functional managers for additional assistance	Perform some alternative analyses and then work with your Program Governance Board to secure their support before you talk with the functional managers	Involve the functional managers as you prepare your resource plan

ELEMENT 4.2 ENSURES PROGRAM ALIGNMENT WITH THE ORGANIZATION'S STRATEGIES

	A	B	C	D
2. Assume your organization recently merged with another company. You now are concerned that the priority of your program in the organization's portfolio may change. You need to:	Strive to set up a meeting with people from the new company to explain your program	Meet regularly with the strategic planners in your organization to gain ongoing support	Ask for a special session of your Program Governance Board for a health check of your program	Meet one-on-one with your key stakeholders to review the program's progress to date

ELEMENT 4.3 WORKS PROACTIVELY WITH THE PROGRAM GOVERNANCE BOARD

	A	B	C	D
3. Realizing the importance of support of your Program Governance Board, a best practice to follow is to:	Ask to have more meetings than those initially scheduled	Prepare a special report outside those in the communications management plan that you can distribute to them each week	Use a decision log to track progress in maintaining your commitments based on their feedback	Accept all of their proposed changes even if you think some may not be appropriate to show you are actively listening to their suggestions

ELEMENT 4.4 PROMOTES OVERALL STAKEHOLDER SUPPORT

	A	B	C	D
4. Assume two of your key stakeholders are having a conflict concerning the future direction of your program. One stakeholder wants another project added to the program, while the other feels it is not necessary. You want to build consensus among them, so you need to:	Demonstrate that you are positive to any and all suggestions	Note that you will adjust the program's vision and revise the business case as needed to meet their concerns	Use strong negotiation skills even if you must use competing or forcing to make a decision	Use objectivity as you meet with them

TOTAL – NEGOTIATING

5.0 Unit of Competence: Thinking Critically

ELEMENT 5.1 CONDUCTS ONGOING ANALYSES TO IDENTIFY TRENDS, VARIANCES, AND ISSUES

	A	B	C	D
1. Assume you regularly analyze your program's metrics to identify any trends, variances, and issues. A best practice to use is:	Environmental scans	Earned value	Brainstorming sessions	Benchmarking forums

ELEMENT 5.2 APPLIES FACT-BASED DECISION MAKING TO CURRENT AND PROSPECTIVE ISSUES

	A	B	C	D
2. In making a decision, you recognize the value of consulting with key stakeholders. This approach can:	Document the source of the decision that is made	Provide an analysis of both assumptions and constraints	Benefit from the use of an influence diagram	Help develop alternatives to consider

ELEMENT 5.3 WORKS PROACTIVELY WITH THE PROGRAM GOVERNANCE STRUCTURE THAT PROVIDES FOR DECISION MAKING AT THE APPROPRIATE LEVELS

	A	B	C	D
3. Assume one of your project managers has an issue on his project, and he has asked you to help him resolve it. You wonder if you can resolve it on your own or if you should involve others. This example shows the importance of:	Stakeholder support	An issue escalation process	The ability to contact your sponsor for guidance at any time	Involving your Program Governance Board in all issues dealing with your program

ELEMENT 5.4 CONSTRUCTIVELY CHALLENGES COMMON BELIEFS AND ASSUMPTIONS – ALWAYS LOOKING FOR A BETTER WAY				
	A	B	C	D
4. Assume on your program that you want to encourage creative thinking and innovation. One approach to follow is to:	Survey your customers for ideas	Make this a requirement in each team member's performance plan and regularly evaluate their effectiveness to do so	Reach out to others not associated with your program	First consult with your sponsor and determine if this is an appropriate practice to follow

TOTAL – THINKING CRITICALLY	

6.0 Unit of Competence: Facilitating

ELEMENT 6.1 PLANS FOR SUCCESS FROM THE START OF THE PROGRAM				
	A	B	C	D
1. One approach to follow to set up an atmosphere focused on program success is to:	Identify and quantify the business benefits	Define some milestones that can be met early in the program	Apply lessons learned from past programs	Hold a kick-off meeting with the team

ELEMENT 6.2 ENSURES THAT ALL TEAM MEMBERS WORK TOGETHER TO ACHIEVE PROGRAM GOALS				
	A	B	C	D
2. One way to get team members to quickly cooperate and collaborate with one another and provide support as required is to:	Use a RAM or RACI chart so everyone understands what each person is responsible for on the program	Set up a process to solicit feedback regularly from the team as to what is working well and what requires change	Link your PWBS to the Resource Breakdown Structure	Combine team development activities with regular meetings and reviews

ELEMENT 6.3 EFFECTIVELY RESOLVES ISSUES TO SOLVE PROBLEMS

	A	B	C	D
3. Because programs are complex undertakings and problems will arise, one approach to resolve issues is to simplify the complexity as much as possible. To do so, you should:	Use techniques to decompose the problem	Hold brainstorming sessions with the stakeholders involved	Show persistence and consistency in your actions to all your stakeholders	Document how the projects and non-project work in the program interrelate so that there are no misunder-standings

ELEMENT 6.4 EFFECTIVELY HANDLES PERSONAL AND TEAM ADVERSITY

	A	B	C	D
4. Because programs are complex, they are a source of stress for many program managers. If you are experiencing stress on your program, an approach to follow is to:	Ask other program managers how they have handled similar situations	Recognize areas in which you need to improve and listen to constructive feedback	Set up a group of peers that you can meet with on a regular basis to discuss ideas with people outside of your program team	Practice a policy of "no surprises"

TOTAL – FACILITATING

7.0 Unit of Competence: Mentoring

ELEMENT 7.1 SUPPORTS MENTORING FOR PROGRAM TEAM MEMBERS

	A	B	C	D
1. My goal as a program manager is to maintain a high level of team motivation. I can best do this by:	Setting up a team-based reward and recognition system	Displaying a genuine, personal interest in each team member	Holding an off-site retreat even if the team is a virtual one	Holding weekly meetings with my team to discuss progress and any areas of concern

ELEMENT 7.2 ESTABLISHES A FORMAL MENTORING PROGRAM				
	A	B	C	D
2. Assume your organization has a mentoring program. Then assume you have two project managers on your program who you believe might benefit from it. The best practice to follow is to:	Assign these two people to others who you believe have shown outstanding success in project management	Offer your own suggestions regularly to these two project managers if you feel they are having any difficulties	Ask the team members if they would like to be linked to a mentor and then help set up goals for the mentoring relationships	Have your entire team meet regularly to discuss problems and areas in which they believe they might benefit from the views of others

ELEMENT 7.3 SUPPORTS INDIVIDUAL AND TEAM DEVELOPMENT ACTIVITIES				
	A	B	C	D
3. As a program manager, it is important to help your team members identify any areas for professional development. One approach is to:	Meet with the individual's functional manager and mutually agree on ways in which each team member can improve	Emphasize the importance of the need for every team member to have certain competencies for overall success in work on your program	Set up an atmosphere that is conducive to creativity and innovation, and recognize individuals for their successes on the program	Provide information about available training opportunities

ELEMENT 7.4 RECOGNIZES AND REWARDS INDIVIDUAL AND TEAM ACCOMPLISHMENTS				
	A	B	C	D
4. Assume on your program that you have a technical subject matter expert who was responsible for a major breakthrough on a key deliverable. You want to recognize this individual for his success. However, you also should:	Recognize others who supported this team member in his or her work	Ask the entire team to personally congratulate this person for his or her contributions	Ensure that the team member's functional group is aware of what this person has accomplished	Capture the intellectual property that has been developed in this initiative
TOTAL – MENTORING				

8.0 Unit of Competence: Embracing Changes			

ELEMENT 8.1 ESTABLISHES AN ENVIRONMENT RECEPTIVE TO CHANGE

	A	B	C	D
1. Because your program spans several years, you know you will have changes to it. You also know most people tend to resist change. You want to promote an approach so people view changes positively. One technique to use is to:	Add a change management specialist to your team for guidance	At various times in the program, make presentations that describe why change is positive and ways to use it to the team's advantage	Set up an easy-to-use process for integrated change control that is not viewed as another layer of bureaucracy by your team members	Ask each team member for his or her own opinions as to his or her personal tolerance for change

ELEMENT 8.2 INFLUENCES FACTORS THAT MAY RESULT IN CHANGE

	A	B	C	D
2. Recognizing that changes will occur on your program, you want to identify factors that could cause change early on to be prepared for it. One approach to use is to:	Add someone to your team who has as his or her main responsibility to survey the external environment and be aware of possible external events that may affect your program	Hold a brainstorming meeting with your core team to identify any possible changes from their perspectives	Survey stakeholders and conduct interviews with them to get their views on events that may result in changes	Prepare and follow a change management plan that includes ways to best identify change

ELEMENT 8.3 PLANS FOR CHANGE AND ITS POTENTIAL IMPACT

	A	B	C	D
3. A change management plan is beneficial for program management. In preparing it, a best practice to follow is to:	Request feedback from stakeholders on a draft plan	Include as part of it the change request process	Ask various stakeholders at appropriate levels if they would be willing to be a member of a Change Control Board	Ask your Program Governance Board members if they wish to also serve as the members of your Change Control Board

ELEMENT 8.4 MANAGES CHANGES WHEN THEY DO OCCUR				
	A	B	C	D
4. To take an action-oriented approach to changes when they occur on your program, you can:	Ask for feedback from your stakeholders as to the approach that you followed when changes occurred for continuous improvement	Document and make available the results of the change impact analysis that was conducted so people can see that action was taken	Model behavior to follow by your team members by personally using the integrated change control system for your program	First, assess any interdependencies of the change with other parts of the program and then follow the change management plan
TOTAL – EMBRACING CHANGES				
TOTAL – ALL PERSONAL COMPETENCIES				

Appendix C1: Answers to Questionnaire in Appendix C

The following contains the answers to the multiple choice questions in Appendix C.

1.0 Defining the Program			

ELEMENT: 1.1 STRATEGIC BENEFITS OF THE PROGRAM ARE UNDERSTOOD BY ALL STAKEHOLDERS

	A	B	C	D
1. Before a program is submitted for possible selection, it is important to analyze the expected benefits of program stakeholders in a:	Benefits statement	**Strategic directive**	Stakeholder log	Prioritized list

ELEMENT 1.2 A PLAN TO INITIATE THE PROGRAM IS PREPARED

	A	B	C	D
2. The document that describes how the program will be initiated is the:	Project charter	Business case	**High-level plan**	Program brief

ELEMENT 1.3 THE PROGRAM'S OBJECTIVES ARE ALIGNED WITH THE STRATEGIC GOALS OF THE ORGANIZATION

	A	B	C	D
3. One criterion to consider when determining whether or not to select a program is to assess its:	Deliverables	Results	**Objectives**	Values

ELEMENT 1.4 A HIGH-LEVEL BUSINESS CASE IS DEVELOPED FOR THE PROGRAM

	A	B	C	D
4. To document the needs, benefits, feasibility, and justification for a program, one should prepare a:	**Business case**	Strategic directive	Mission statement	Program vision

ELEMENT 1.5 A NUMBER OF GATES OR STAGES ARE IDENTIFIED WHEN PROGRAM STATUS (INCLUDING BENEFIT REALIZATION) WILL BE REVIEWED

	A	B	C	D
5. In order to determine whether or not a program is on track, one should use:	Milestones	**Gates**	Portfolio management	Forecasts

TOTAL – DEFINING

2.0 Initiating the Program			

ELEMENT 2.1 A PROGRAM CHARTER IS PREPARED

	A	B	C	D
1. The document, when approved, that is used to move to the Program Set Up phase is the:	Business case	High-level plan	Program roadmap	**Program charter**

ELEMENT 2.2 THE PROGRAM VISION IS DOCUMENTED TO SHOW THE END STATE AND ITS BENEFIT TO THE ORGANIZATION

	A	B	C	D
2. The end state of the program is its:	**Vision**	Mission	Deliverables	Results

ELEMENT 2.3 KEY PROGRAM DECISION MAKERS ARE IDENTIFIED

	A	B	C	D
3. The executive sponsor and the program manager are appointed during which phase in the program management life cycle?	Pre-program preparations	**Program initiation**	Program set up	Defining

ELEMENT 2.4 STAKEHOLDER EXPECTATIONS AND INTERESTS ARE IDENTIFIED

	A	B	C	D
4. The link between business strategy and planned or unplanned work is part of the:	Business case	Charter	**Roadmap**	High-level plan

ELEMENT 2.5 HIGH-LEVEL RISKS TO THE PROGRAM ARE IDENTIFIED

	A	B	C	D
5. One approach to consider in identifying high-level risks is use of a:	Probability matrix	Decision tree	Sensitivity analysis	**SWOT analysis**

ELEMENT 2.6 CANDIDATE PROJECTS TO BE IN THE PROGRAM, AS WELL AS NON-PROJECT WORK, ARE IDENTIFIED

	A	B	C	D
6. The document that shows how components are organized by stages or blocks is the:	Architecture	**Roadmap**	Prioritized list	Business case

ELEMENT 2.7 AN INITIAL INFRASTRUCTURE FOR PROGRAM MANAGEMENT IS DETERMINED

	A	B	C	D
7. A high-level snapshot of the program's infrastructure is contained in the:	Program charter	Business case	PMO charter	**Roadmap**

ELEMENT 2.8 THE TIMETABLE TO COMPLETE THE PROGRAM IS DETERMINED

	A	B	C	D
8. An order-of-magnitude schedule is prepared during which of the following phases in the program management life cycle?	**Program initiation**	Pre-program preparations	Program set up	Initiate program

ELEMENT 2.9 INITIAL ESTIMATES OF THE PROGRAM'S COST ARE PREPARED

	A	B	C	D
9. An initial cost estimate is contained in the program's:	Governance plan	**Financial framework**	Cost management plan	Project charter

ELEMENT 2.10 KEY RESOURCES FOR PROGRAM MANAGEMENT ARE IDENTIFIED TO SET UP THE PROGRAM

	A	B	C	D
10. For the initial stages of the program, you should prepare a list of required resources. This is done by preparing a (an):	Budget estimate	Resource plan	**Order-of-magnitude estimate**	Resource baseline

ELEMENT 2.11 THE PROGRAM CHARTER IS APPROVED

	A	B	C	D
11. The program charter is approved and signed off by:	The sponsor	The executive director	The program manager	**The Program Governance Board**

TOTAL – INITIATING

3.0 Planning the Program

ELEMENT 3.1 A PROGRAM MANAGEMENT PLAN IS PREPARED

	A	B	C	D
1. The key elements of program direction and management are contained in the:	**Program management plan**	Program execution plan	Program manager's charter	Program roadmap

ELEMENT 3.2 A BENEFITS REALIZATION PLAN IS PREPARED

	A	B	C	D
2. Metrics to use to track progress in benefits delivery are contained in the:	Program performance reports	**Benefits realization plan**	Benefits realization report	Program requirements document

ELEMENT 3.3 KEY PROGRAM RISKS AND ISSUES ARE IDENTIFIED

	A	B	C	D
3. One approach to follow to identify key program risks is to:	Define risk profiles	Discuss risks at each meeting of your Program Governance Board	Determine risk tolerances	**Hold a risk planning meeting**

ELEMENT 3.4 THE PROGRAM'S BUDGET IS DETERMINED

	A	B	C	D
4. Analyzing your program's operational costs is useful in:	**Preparing the program's financial plan**	Determining the funding goals	Preparing the financial framework	Documenting a payment schedule

ELEMENT 3.5 DEPENDENCIES, CONSTRAINTS, AND ASSUMPTIONS ARE DOCUMENTED

	A	B	C	D
5. Program assumptions and constraints are documented in the program's:	Requirements document	Scope management plan	**Scope statement**	PWBS dictionary

ELEMENT 3.6 A STRATEGY TO MANAGE THE PROGRAM AND ITS COMPONENTS IS AGREED UPON AND DOCUMENTED

	A	B	C	D
6. One approach to foster control and communications with those in a program who are managing projects and non-project work is to prepare a:	Program vision	Program charter	**PWBS**	Statement of objectives

ELEMENT 3.7 NECESSARY FEASIBILITY STUDIES ARE CONDUCTED

	A	B	C	D
7. One reason it is necessary to assess market environmental factors is that they may:	Affect the change management plan	**Lead to changes not documented in the business case**	Require review of the charter	Change the program manager's responsibilities

ELEMENT 3.8 A ROADMAP OR ARCHITECTURE TO SHOW THE INTERRELATIONSHIPS AMONG THE COMPONENT PROJECTS AND NON-PROJECT WORK IN THE PROGRAM IS PREPARED

	A	B	C	D
8. As new projects become part of the program, you should, among other things:	Document the program's vision	Document the program's values	Baseline the architecture	**Update the roadmap**

ELEMENT 3.9 A COMMUNICATIONS STRATEGY FOR EACH STAKEHOLDER IS DETERMINED

	A	B	C	D
9. The scope statement, among other things, shows stakeholder acceptance criteria, but stakeholders should:	Participate in developing the stakeholder management plan	**Sign off on deliverables and benefits**	Receive a copy of the stakeholder management strategy	Receive updates when the register changes

ELEMENT 3.10 A PROGRAM MANAGEMENT OFFICE (PMO) IS APPROVED AND IMPLEMENTED				
	A	B	C	D
10. Program management elements and artifacts to use should be included in the:	**PWBS**	Scope statement	Program charter	Requirements document

ELEMENT 3.11 TOOLS, PROCESSES, AND TECHNIQUES REQUIRED FOR PROGRAM MANAGEMENT ARE OBTAINED				
	A	B	C	D
11. One approach to manage program data and information is to:	Prepare a program reporting plan	Use the same status reports for all stakeholders	Use the EPMO	**Establish a PMIS**

ELEMENT 3.12 THE PROGRAM MANAGEMENT PLAN IS APPROVED				
	A	B	C	D
12. The program management plan must be approved before moving to which phase in the program life cycle?	Executing	Program set up	**Delivery of program benefits**	Set up the program and technical infrastructure

ELEMENT 3.13 A PROGRAM MANAGEMENT GOVERNANCE STRUCTURE IS DETERMINED				
	A	B	C	D
13. Key governance roles and responsibilities are included in the:	Program architecture	**Governance plan**	PMO charter	Program roadmap

ELEMENT 3.14 A PROGRAM CONTROL FRAMEWORK IS ESTABLISHED TO ASSIST IN BENEFIT MEASUREMENT AS WELL AS IN OVERALL MANAGEMENT OF THE PROGRAM'S COMPONENTS				
	A	B	C	D
14. The basis for future program decisions is one purpose of the:	**Scope statement**	Performance plan	Business case	Program charter

TOTAL – PLANNING

4.0 Executing the Program

ELEMENT 4.1 PROJECTS ARE INITIATED AS PART OF THE PROGRAM				
	A	B	C	D
1. In order to initiate a new project for my program, I should first:	Prepare a project charter	Contact my sponsor	**Prepare a business case**	Meet with the Program Governance Board

ELEMENT 4.2 SHARED RESOURCES REQUIRED FOR COMPONENT PROJECTS THE NON-PROJECT WORK ARE COORDINATED				
	A	B	C	D
2. One important use of the PMIS is to:	**Identify resource issues early**	Show the changes required	Prepare a resource plan	Validate time reporting

ELEMENT 4.3 CHANGE REQUESTS ARE REVIEWED

	A	B	C	D
3. When one project on my program has a change, I then need to, as the program manager:	Authorize it	**Determine its impact on other parts of the program**	Convene a meeting of the Change Control Board (CCB)	Meet with the Program Governance Board

ELEMENT 4.4 ADDITIONAL WORK IS AUTHORIZED AS REQUIRED

	A	B	C	D
4. Assume there is a change on my program, as part of the decision-making structure that is set up, as the program manager, I should then:	Immediately recognize changes in priorities	Update the program charter	**Know when to escalate it to the Program Governance Board**	Update all of my plans

ELEMENT 4.5 COMMUNICATIONS WITH STAKEHOLDERS IS FOSTERED AND ENCOURAGED AT ALL LEVELS

	A	B	C3	D
5. Metrics to show stakeholder engagement activities are included in the stakeholder:	Inventory	Management strategy	Register	**Management plan**

ELEMENT 4.6 COMMUNICATIONS WITH MEMBERS OF THE PROGRAM GOVERNANCE BOARD OCCURS ON A REGULAR BASIS

	A	B	C	D
6. Often, during meetings with members of my Program Governance Board, I provide them with:	**An update of the budget baseline**	The stakeholder register	The communications log	The team's RACI or RAM chart

ELEMENT 4.7 ALIGNMENT OF THE PROGRAM'S GOALS, AND ITS BENEFITS, IS ASSESSED AGAINST THAT OF THE ORGANIZATION

	A	B	C	D
7. Because organizational priorities may change during the life of a program, I tend to document and update, when needed:	Minutes from Program Governance Board meetings	**Links from each project to the organization's strategic goals**	Ad hoc communications with stakeholders	Results from health checks and maturity assessments

ELEMENT 4.8 COMMON ACTIVITIES OF THE PROGRAM'S PROJECTS AND NON-PROJECT WORK ARE COORDINATED

	A	B	C	D
8. One way I make sure that common activities of the components of my program are coordinated is to:	Document minutes from meetings with components	Use the PMO	Suggest updates to corporate policies	**Follow the communications management plan**

ELEMENT 4.9 DEPENDENCIES WITH OTHER ORGANIZATIONAL INITIATIVES ARE COORDINATED

	A	B	C	D
9. I conduct lessons learned meetings, and also I:	Establish an organizational knowledge management system	**Maintain a lessons learned database**	Establish a benefits management system	Update specific project plans that are part of the program

ELEMENT 4.10 THE PROGRAM MANAGEMENT PLAN IS EXECUTED

	A	B	C	D
10. You want to show your program's benefits have been delivered so you should:	Rebaseline your benefits realization plan	Update your reports	Update your communications management plan	**Document completion of your deliverables**

TOTAL – EXECUTING

5.0 Monitoring and Controlling the Program

ELEMENT 5.1 PROGRESS IS ANALYZED ACCORDING TO THE PROGRAM MANAGEMENT PLAN

	A	B	C	D
1. Assume you are using a number of suppliers on your program. You then need to analyze their performance and you can do so by:	**Conducting supplier reviews**	Using suppliers that are on the organization's qualified seller list	Including suppliers in meetings with your team	Establishing partnering agreements from the beginning to minimize possible claims or disputes

ELEMENT 5.2 BENEFIT REALIZATION IS ANALYZED ACCORDING TO THE BENEFITS REALIZATION PLAN

	A	B	C	D
2. Benefits realization analysis is a tool and technique that is used to:	Determine if the life-cycle costs will exceed the benefits to be realized	**Ensure the program delivers the promised benefits and that they translate into value**	Assess the value of the benefits realization report based on a survey of stakeholders	Conduct an effective benefits review

ELEMENT 5.3 ISSUES AND RISKS ARE CONTINUOUSLY IDENTIFIED, AND CORRECTIVE ACTIONS ARE TAKEN AS REQUIRED

	A	B	C	D
3. One way I provide oversight of risks on my program is to:	Continually identify risks at the project and program levels	Regularly update each project's risk management plan	Set up trigger conditions for risks at the program and individual project levels	**Use risk audits**

ELEMENT 5.4 EXTERNAL ENVIRONMENTAL CHANGES ARE ANALYZED TO DETERMINE THE POSSIBLE IMPACT ON THE PROGRAM AND ITS REALIZATION OF BENEFITS

	A	B	C	D
4. Assume you are managing a complex program. It has the possibility of a class action lawsuit. This means you should:	Have a member from your legal department on your core team	**Monitor legal issues**	Ensure you have continual governance oversight	Set up an issue resolution process and follow it throughout your program

ELEMENT 5.5 GOVERNANCE OVERSIGHT IS REGULARLY PRACTICED AT THE PROGRAM AND PROJECT LEVELS

	A	B	C	D
5. One way I make sure I am following suggestions from my Program Governance Board is that I use a:	**Governance decision register**	Governance tracking log	Governance report	Governance performance plan

ELEMENT 5.6 PROGRAM CHANGES ARE IMPLEMENTED IN ACCORDANCE WITH ESTABLISHED INTEGRATED CHANGE CONTROL PROCEDURES

	A	B	C	D
6. A best practice that I would follow on my program is to first use:	**A change request form for each proposed change**	A change request log	An integrated change control process	A meeting of the Change Control Board (CCB)

ELEMENT 5.7 PROGRAM EXECUTION IS MONITORED ACCORDING TO THE PROGRAM MANAGEMENT PLAN

	A	B	C	D
7. One approach I would use on a program to predict the likelihood of achieving my planned outcomes is:	Trend analysis	Regular status reporting	**Earned value**	PMIS

ELEMENT 5.8 SCHEDULE SLIPPAGES AND OPPORTUNITIES ARE IDENTIFIED AND MANAGED

	A	B	C	D
8. We tend to focus our emphasis in schedule control on ways in which we can make up any delays that have occurred on our programs. But attention also is needed on documenting:	Preventive actions	Minutes from supplier reviews	**Opportunities to accelerate the schedule**	The Complete Performance Index

ELEMENT 5.9 PROACTIVE COST CONTROL IS FOLLOWED

	A	B	C	D
9. In analyzing the work of suppliers on a program, a best practice to follow for potential cost impact is to:	**Establish a budget management system**	Conduct a variance analysis	Conduct lessons learned sessions	Use benchmarking data

ELEMENT 5.10 STAKEHOLDER EXPECTATIONS ARE MANAGED

	A	B	C	D
10. Assume you have over 100 different stakeholders on your program and have set up 12 stakeholder groups for effective management. You want to make sure all stakeholders participate, so you should:	Set up leads for each of the groups and meet with them one-on-one weekly or biweekly	**Use a stakeholder communications log**	Survey each stakeholder monthly for ideas	Make sure all stakeholders receive the same information regardless of whether they are internal or external

ELEMENT 5.11 PERFORMANCE DATA ARE CONSOLIDATED TO DETERMINE APPROPRIATE RESOURCE USE TO DELIVER BENEFITS

	A	B	C	D
11. On my program, each time I hold a status review meeting, I:	Communicate the results to all my stakeholders	Notify all my stakeholders in advance so they can attend even if they do so virtually	**Document minutes and action items**	Ensure that each person who attends has an opportunity to speak

ELEMENT 5.12 COMPONENTS TRANSITION TO CLOSURE

	A	B	C	D
12. Before closing a project on my program, I:	Evaluate team member performance	Reallocate resources to other projects or other parts of the organization	Dismantle the PMO	**Document a request to close the project and present it to the Program Governance Board**

TOTAL– MONITORING AND CONTROLLING

6.0 Closing the Program

ELEMENT 6.1 THE PROGRAM IS FORMALLY CLOSED

	A	B	C	D
1. In closing my program, it is necessary to close its financial activities. As a program manager, a major activity to perform is to:	Conduct a final earned value analysis	Finalize the budget baseline	Meet with the financial department to discuss lessons learned	**Provide a full-scope verification audit and accounting of financial records**

ELEMENT 6.2 PRODUCTS AND SERVICES TRANSITION TO OPERATIONS

	A	B	C	D
2. Before my program can transition to operations, it is important to ensure that:	**Documented acceptance from operations is obtained**	The same core team will work with operations	The program has met all business case deliverables	The benefits realization report is finalized

ELEMENT 6.3 PROGRAM BENEFITS ARE REALIZED

	A	B	C	D
3. One way to ensure that all the benefits in the program have been realized is to:	Compare the realized benefits with those stated during the benefits identification stage of the benefits life cycle	**Meet with stakeholders to discuss any outstanding issues**	Evaluate the realized benefits with those listed in the business case	Receive formal approval from all Program Governance Board members

ELEMENT 6.4 CUSTOMER SUPPORT IS PROVIDED (AS APPLICABLE, SUCH AS DEFINED IN A CONTRACT)				
	A	B	C	D
4. Assume your program was handled through a contract. Future maintenance support is:	Handled as an additional procurement	Contained in the RFP	**Detailed in the contract**	Provided as discussed and documented with your customer

ELEMENT 6.5 LESSONS LEARNED ARE INTEGRATED INTO THE ORGANIZATION'S KNOWLEDGE MANAGEMENT SYSTEM				
	A	B	C	D
5. On my program, I publish lessons learned and incorporate them into the:	**Final report**	Knowledge management system	Final review with the sponsor	Final review with the team

ELEMENT 6.6 FEEDBACK IS PROVIDED ON AREAS OUTSIDE THE SCOPE OF THE PROGRAM				
	A	B	C	D
6. On my program, one of my team members discussed a lesson learned, but it did not affect our program. I then:	Placed it in the knowledge repository for this program for future reference	Suggested the team member consider it on the next program or project	**Provided it to our Enterprise Program Management Office (EPMO) to pass on to other programs and projects**	Discussed it with our program stakeholders

ELEMENT 6.7 PROGRAM DOCUMENTS ARE ARCHIVED FOR FUTURE REUSE				
	A	B	C	D
7. In closing the program, I have asked my core team to archive program documents. They should, as a best practice:	Place them in the knowledge repository	Set up a discussion forum to discuss them before formal closure	Survey the entire team for areas of future improvement	**Index them**

ELEMENT 6.8 CONTRACTUAL OBLIGATIONS ARE MET				
	A	B	C	D
8. In finalizing the procurement aspects of my program, it is important to:	Conduct an audit of each contract	**Document sign-offs by our organization and the supplier**	Include all aspects of the contract in the final archives	Document preventive actions

ELEMENT 6.9 INTELLECTUAL PROPERTY IS CAPTURED FOR REUSE				
	A	B	C	D
9. It is critical to reuse intellectual property gained on the program. But, in doing so, as a program manager:	**Confidentiality agreements should be followed**	Interviews should be held with standard questions with all team members before they leave the team	Emphasize that the intellectual property only remain with the team itself	Interface actively with the Knowledge Management Office

ELEMENT 6.10 A LEGACY OF BENEFIT SUSTAINMENT IS ACHIEVED				
	A	B	C	D
10. At the end of each program, as the program manager, it is important to make sure the products and services of the program add value. This can best be done by:	Documenting user experience	**Verifying support for the new product or service**	Surveying the program's stakeholders	Setting up a new life cycle to focus more on benefit sustainment
TOTAL – CLOSING				
TOTAL – ALL PERFORMANCE COMPETENCIES				

These questions involve personal competencies.

1.0 Communicating			

ELEMENT: 1.1 ACTIVELY LISTENS, UNDERSTANDS, AND RESPONDS TO STAKEHOLDERS

	A	B	C	D
1. If I find that I am not paying as much close attention as I should to some of the stakeholders when I am talking with them, I should:	Make sure communications are reciprocal and are not one-sided	Track each message	Use a communications log	**Request that the speaker repeat the information if I do not clearly understand it**

ELEMENT 1.2 USES THE KEY CHANNELS OF COMMUNICATIONS

	A	B	C	D
2. Both informal and formal communications are useful. Informal communications are preferred for:	**Day-to-day activities**	Results from meetings	Overall program status	Surveys

ELEMENT 1.3 ENSURES THE QUALITY OF THE INFORMATION THAT IS COMMUNICATED

	A	B	C	D
3. Program information should be accurate and factual. At times, however, it should be validated by:	Program Governance Board members	**Experts**	Use of the Delphi Technique	Team members

ELEMENT 1.4 TAILORS THE INFORMATION TO THE AUDIENCE

	A	B	C	D
4. As a program manager, it is important to determine the most suitable approach to communicate with each stakeholder group. To do so, you should:	Use the stakeholder inventory	Follow the program's information distribution process	**Use the stakeholder analysis**	Use the stakeholder register

ELEMENT 1.5 EFFECTIVELY USES EACH OF THE COMMUNICATIONS DIMENSIONS

	A	B	C	D
5. Assume you are meeting with your team. To make sure everyone speaks up, one approach to use is to:	Discuss each topic and have everyone make a comment on it even if it is a repeat	Use "I" messages	Explain in advance that everyone is expected to actively participate	**Ask open-ended questions**

TOTAL – COMMUNICATING

2.0 Unit of Competence: Leading			

ELEMENT 2.1 IMPLEMENTS THE PROGRAM'S VISION

	A	B	C	D
1. To describe the vision of the program to my team, I:	Refer them to the program charter	**Hold a kick-off meeting**	Provide each team member with a copy of it	Talk with each team member one-on-one to discuss it

ELEMENT 2.2 ESTABLISHES THE PROGRAM'S DIRECTION

	A	B	C	D
2. One way to determine the program's critical success factors is to:	Review the business case	Ask the program sponsor and other stakeholders	**Use a Delphi Technique**	Use the program roadmap

ELEMENT 2.3 RECOGNIZES THE INTERDEPENDENCIES WITHIN THE PROGRAM

	A	B	C	D
3. One approach to determine how the projects and the non-project work in the programs interface is to:	**Prepare a component analysis**	Review each of the project plans in depth	Conduct a comparative advantage analysis	Conduct a feasibility study

ELEMENT 2.4 TAKES CALCULATED RISKS; IS VENTURESOME

	A	B	C	D
4. You have decided to take risks on new ideas that seem promising. One approach to follow is to:	**Conduct a risk vs. opportunity analysis meeting with your team**	Use corrective action	Use preventive actions	Use focus groups

ELEMENT 2.5 ASSUMES OWNERSHIP FOR THE PROGRAM

	A	B	C	D
5. As the program manager, you are responsible for the program's success. One way to demonstrate your ownership of the program is:	Active involvement with stakeholders, especially those external to the program	Maintaining a priority list of action items	Including project managers in meetings with the Program Governance Board at key stage gates	**Active involvement with stakeholders, especially members of the Program Governance Board**

TOTAL – LEADING				

3.0 Unit of Competence: Building Relationships			

ELEMENT 3.1 BUILDS TRUST AMONG STAKEHOLDERS, CLIENTS, AND TEAM MEMBERS

	A	B	C	D
1. You realize that some stakeholders will be more actively involved in the program while others may only have a peripheral interest in it. You should assess:	Their opinions about the program	**Their ability to influence or impact the program**	The types or groups of stakeholders who will be involved to some degree	Which team member is best suited to work individually to ensure that the stakeholder's expectations are met

ELEMENT 3.2 LEVERAGES THE ORGANIZATION'S POLITICAL DYNAMICS TO PROMOTE PROGRAM GOALS

	A	B	C	D
2. You realize the importance of recognizing the internal dynamics of your organization. This means you should:	**Review organizational charts and note key interfaces with the EPMO**	Determine mitigation approaches to outline steps to take to manage the impact of the program on stakeholders	Review external environmental factors that may affect the program	Assess information as to likely stakeholder responses to the actions you take as program manager

ELEMENT 3.3 ADVOCATES FOR DIVERSITY AND TREATS OTHERS WITH COURTESY AND RESPECT

	A	B	C	D
3. Your goal is to have a diverse program team. Therefore, you should:	Use the organization's knowledge, skills, and competency profiles	Make sure that everyone on the team is motivated the same way, regardless of their different backgrounds	**Establish a team that consists of people with different backgrounds and points of view**	Prepare an Equal Opportunity Employment Plan

ELEMENT 3.4 ESTABLISHES AND DEMONSTRATES HIGH STANDARDS FOR PERSONAL AND TEAM MEMBER PERFORMANCE				
	A	B	C	D
4. I realize as a program manager the importance of setting up individual performance goals and standards. A best practice to follow is to:	Evaluate performance using a 360-degree approach	**Link these individual goals to the overall program goals and objectives**	Make sure each of my team member's personal goals are congruent with my own personal goals	Prepare an individual development plan and provide it to each team member

ELEMENT 3.5 PROMOTES AND DEMONSTRATES ETHICS, INTEGRITY, AND ADHERENCE TO CORPORATE VALUES IN ALL INTERACTIONS				
	A	B	C	D
5. Assume that on your team you want to make sure everyone understands his or her ethical responsibilities. You should:	**Have each team member sign an ethics or conflict-of-interest statement**	Enforce your ethics code	Make the ethics code a part of each team member's performance plan and evaluate performance against it	Prepare an ethics plan as your first step
TOTAL – BUILDING RELATIONSHIPS				

4.0 Unit of Competence: Negotiating			
ELEMENT 4.1 OBTAINS NEEDED PROGRAM RESOURCES			
	A	B	C	D

	A	B	C	D
1. Most program managers must obtain resources from functional managers. For effectiveness in this area, a best practice to follow is to:	Prepare a staffing management plan for your program and ask for comments from the functional managers	Use subject matter experts as you negotiate for resources with the functional managers for additional assistance	Perform some alternative analyses and then work with your Program Governance Board to secure their support before you talk with the functional managers	**Involve the functional managers as you prepare your resource plan**

ELEMENT 4.2 ENSURES PROGRAM ALIGNMENT WITH THE ORGANIZATION'S STRATEGIES

	A	B	C	D
2. Assume your organization recently merged with another company. You now are concerned that the priority of your program in the organization's portfolio may change. You need to:	Strive to set up a meeting with people from the new company to explain your program	**Meet regularly with the strategic planners in your organization to gain ongoing support**	Ask for a special session of your Program Governance Board for a health check of your program	Meet one-on-one with your key stakeholders to review the program's progress to date

ELEMENT 4.3 WORKS PROACTIVELY WITH THE PROGRAM GOVERNANCE BOARD

	A	B	C	D
3. Realizing the importance of support of your Program Governance Board, a best practice to follow is to:	Ask to have more meetings than those initially scheduled	Prepare a special report outside those in the communications management plan that you can distribute to them each week	**Use a decision log to track progress in maintaining your commitments based on their feedback**	Accept all of their proposed changes even if you think some may not be appropriate to show you are actively listening to their suggestions

ELEMENT 4.4 PROMOTES OVERALL STAKEHOLDER SUPPORT

	A	B	C	D
4. Assume two of your key stakeholders are having a conflict concerning the future direction of your program. One stakeholder wants another project added to the program, while the other feels it is not necessary. You want to build consensus among them, so you need to:	Demonstrate that you are positive to any and all suggestions	Note that you will adjust the program's vision and revise the business case as needed to meet their concerns	Use strong negotiation skills even if you must use competing or forcing to make a decision	**Use objectivity as you meet with them**

TOTAL – NEGOTIATING

5.0 Unit of Competence: Thinking Critically

ELEMENT 5.1 CONDUCTS ONGOING ANALYSES TO IDENTIFY TRENDS, VARIANCES, AND ISSUES

	A	B	C	D
1. Assume you regularly analyze your program's metrics to identify any trends, variances, and issues. A best practice to use is:	Environmental scans	**Earned value**	Brainstorming sessions	Benchmarking forums

ELEMENT 5.2 APPLIES FACT-BASED DECISION MAKING TO CURRENT AND PROSPECTIVE ISSUES

	A	B	C	D
2. In making a decision, you recognize the value of consulting with key stakeholders. This approach can:	Document the source of the decision that is made	Provide an analysis of both assumptions and constraints	Benefit from the use of an influence diagram	**Help develop alternatives to consider**

ELEMENT 5.3 WORKS PROACTIVELY WITH THE PROGRAM GOVERNANCE STRUCTURE THAT PROVIDES FOR DECISION MAKING AT THE APPROPRIATE LEVELS

	A	B	C	D
3. Assume one of your project managers has an issue on his project, and he has asked you to help him resolve it. You wonder if you can resolve it on your own or if you should involve others. This example shows the importance of:	Stakeholder support	**An issue escalation process**	The ability to contact your sponsor for guidance at any time	Involving your Program Governance Board in all issues dealing with your program

ELEMENT 5.4 CONSTRUCTIVELY CHALLENGES COMMON BELIEFS AND ASSUMPTIONS – ALWAYS LOOKING FOR A BETTER WAY

	A	B	C	D
4. Assume on your program that you want to encourage creative thinking and innovation. One approach to follow is to:	Survey your customers for ideas	Make this a requirement in each team member's performance plan and regularly evaluate their effectiveness to do so	**Reach out to others not associated with your program**	First consult with your sponsor and determine if this is an appropriate practice to follow

TOTAL – THINKING CRITICALLY

6.0 Unit of Competence: Facilitating

ELEMENT 6.1 PLANS FOR SUCCESS FROM THE START OF THE PROGRAM

	A	B	C	D
1. One approach to follow to set up an atmosphere focused on program success is to:	Identify and quantify the business benefits	**Define some milestones that can be met early in the program**	Apply lessons learned from past programs	Hold a kick-off meeting with the team

ELEMENT 6.2 ENSURES THAT ALL TEAM MEMBERS WORK TOGETHER TO ACHIEVE PROGRAM GOALS

	A	B	C	D
2. One way to get team members to quickly cooperate and collaborate with one another and provide support as required is to:	Use a RAM or RACI chart so everyone understands what each person is responsible for on the program	Set up a process to solicit feedback regularly from the team as to what is working well and what requires change	Link your PWBS to the Resource Breakdown Structure	**Combine team development activities with regular meetings and reviews**

ELEMENT 6.3 EFFECTIVELY RESOLVES ISSUES TO SOLVE PROBLEMS

	A	B	C	D
3. Because programs are complex undertakings and problems will arise, one approach to resolve issues is to simplify the complexity as much as possible. To do so, you should:	**Use techniques to decompose the problem**	Hold brainstorming sessions with the stakeholders involved	Show persistence and consistency in your actions to all your stakeholders	Document how the projects and non-project work in the program interrelate so that there are no misunder-standings

ELEMENT 6.4 EFFECTIVELY HANDLES PERSONAL AND TEAM ADVERSITY

	A	B	C	D
4. Because programs are complex, they are a source of stress for many program managers. If you are experiencing stress on your program, an approach to follow is to:	Ask other program managers how they have handled similar situations	**Recognize areas in which you need to improve and listen to constructive feedback**	Set up a group of peers that you can meet with on a regular basis to discuss ideas with people outside of your program team	Practice a policy of "no surprises"

TOTAL – FACILITATING

7.0 Unit of Competence: Mentoring

ELEMENT 7.1 SUPPORTS MENTORING FOR PROGRAM TEAM MEMBERS

	A	B	C	D
1. My goal as a program manager is to maintain a high level of team motivation. I can best do this by:	Setting up a team-based reward and recognition system	**Displaying a genuine, personal interest in each team member**	Holding an off-site retreat even if the team is a virtual one	Holding weekly meetings with my team to discuss progress and any areas of concern

ELEMENT 7.2 ESTABLISHES A FORMAL MENTORING PROGRAM

	A	B	C	D
2. Assume your organization has a mentoring program. Then assume you have two project managers on your program who you believe might benefit from it. The best practice to follow is to:	Assign these two people to others who you believe have shown outstanding success in project management	Offer your own suggestions regularly to these two project managers if you feel they are having any difficulties	**Ask the team members if they would like to be linked to a mentor and then help set up goals for the mentoring relationships**	Have your entire team meet regularly to discuss problems and areas in which they believe they might benefit from the views of others

ELEMENT 7.3 SUPPORTS INDIVIDUAL AND TEAM DEVELOPMENT ACTIVITIES

	A	B	C	D
3. As a program manager, it is important to help your team members identify any areas for professional development. One approach is to:	Meet with the individual's functional manager and mutually agree on ways in which each team member can improve	Emphasize the importance of the need for every team member to have certain competencies for overall success in work on your program	Set up an atmosphere that is conducive to creativity and innovation, and recognize individuals for their successes on the program	**Provide information about available training opportunities**

ELEMENT 7.4 RECOGNIZES AND REWARDS INDIVIDUAL AND TEAM ACCOMPLISHMENTS

	A	B	C	D
4. Assume on your program that you have a technical subject matter expert who was responsible for a major breakthrough on a key deliverable. You want to recognize this individual for his success. However, you also should:	**Recognize others who supported this team member in his or her work**	Ask the entire team to personally congratulate this person for his or her contributions	Ensure that the team member's functional group is aware of what this person has accomplished	Capture the intellectual property that has been developed in this initiative

TOTAL – MENTORING

8.0 Unit of Competence: Embracing Changes			

ELEMENT 8.1 ESTABLISHES AN ENVIRONMENT RECEPTIVE TO CHANGE

	A	B	C	D
1. Because your program spans several years, you know you will have changes to it. You also know most people tend to resist change. You want to promote an approach so people view changes positively. One technique to use is to:	Add a change management specialist to your team for guidance	**At various times in the program, make presentations that describe why change is positive and ways to use it to the team's advantage**	Set up an easy-to-use process for integrated change control that is not viewed as another layer of bureaucracy by your team members	Ask each team member for his or her own opinions as to his or her personal tolerance for change

ELEMENT 8.2 INFLUENCES FACTORS THAT MAY RESULT IN CHANGE

	A	B	C	D
2. Recognizing that changes will occur on your program, you want to identify factors that could cause change early on to be prepared for it. One approach to use is to:	Add someone to your team who has as his or her main responsibility to survey the external environment and be aware of possible external events that may affect your program	Hold a brainstorming meeting with your core team to identify any possible changes from their perspectives	**Survey stakeholders and conduct interviews with them to get their views on events that may result in changes**	Prepare and follow a change management plan that includes ways to best identify change

ELEMENT 8.3 PLANS FOR CHANGE AND ITS POTENTIAL IMPACT

	A	B	C	D
3. A change management plan is beneficial for program management. In preparing it, a best practice to follow is to:	**Request feedback from stakeholders on a draft plan**	Include as part of it the change request process	Ask various stakeholders at appropriate levels if they would be willing to be a member of a Change Control Board	Ask your Program Governance Board members if they wish to also serve as the members of your Change Control Board

ELEMENT 8.4 MANAGES CHANGES WHEN THEY DO OCCUR				
	A	B	C	D
4. To take an action-oriented approach to changes when they occur on your program, you can:	**Ask for feedback from your stakeholders as to the approach that you followed when changes occurred for continuous improvement**	Document and make available the results of the change impact analysis that was conducted so people can see that action was taken	Model behavior to follow by your team members by personally using the integrated change control system for your program	First, assess any interdependencies of the change with other parts of the program and then follow the change management plan
TOTAL – EMBRACING CHANGES				
TOTAL – ALL PERSONAL COMPETENCIES				

Appendix D: A Suggested Project Plan for Implementing the Levin-Ward Program Management Complexity Model

The authors have planned and executed numerous assessments for many companies and government agencies around the world; and we have conducted assessments at the individual as well as the organizational levels. The best assessments are planned and executed as a "project" with a project manager and core and extended teams supported by an executive sponsor. Accordingly, we have developed many project plans for such assessments to help our clients implement them as quickly and easily as possible. We have included a "generic" plan that you can use to help get started. If you develop a plan and stick to it, chances are you are well on your way to a successful assessment.

So that you can quickly and easily implement our model, which is done through the questionnaires included in this book, we have included the following "generic" project plan, replete with all the necessary tasks, to get you started.

Task 1: Define User Requirements:
- Define the "respondent" population.
- Create e-mail distribution lists.

- Define scope of assessment.
- Define the demographics section of the survey to ensure assessment data can be segregated by various fields such as country, title, business unit, division, certification achieved, training completed, or other relevant qualifying information.

Task 2: Customize Survey Content:
- In addition to the questions included in each questionnaire in this book, you may want to include additional questions that address such areas as methodology use, applying key best practices, adherence to stated practices and procedures, or other areas where you are interested in collecting data on performance. (Note: the authors do not advise changing or modifying the questions in the questionnaires in this book as considerable time and effort were spent to develop questions that address the model.)

Task 3: Develop Online Survey
- Develop the online survey (i.e., taking the questions from this book and putting them into the survey tool of choice).
- Send link to the organization's project contacts for review and feedback (this step is a quality control function to make sure the link works, the survey questions are on target, and the survey tool is working with no problems).
- Refine survey questions (i.e., any of the additional ones added to the Levin-Ward questionnaires).

Task 4: Deploy Survey:
- Survey invitation: an e-mail is sent to the identified respondents asking them to take the survey within a specific time period (we recommend two weeks). The e-mail includes a link to the survey tool, and a contact name and e-mail address if they have any questions. Additionally, the e-mail will explain the purpose of the survey and technical instructions for taking the survey.
- Survey Reminder: approximately ten days after the survey invitation is sent, a reminder e-mail is distributed to

the respondents reminding them to take the survey if they have not already done so.

- Survey "Thank you": approximately two days after the survey end date, a thank-you e-mail is sent to each respondent expressing appreciation for their time in taking the survey.

Task 5: Data Analysis and Evaluation:
- Conduct data analysis.
- Write a draft analysis report: the report is typically subdivided into several sections to include findings, interpretation of findings, and recommendations for improvement. Additionally, the most useful and usable report will identify a roadmap, with suggested key dates, when stated improvements will commence.
- Review and comment on analysis report.
- Write the final analysis report.
- Develop a presentation of findings.
- Present findings to key stakeholders and other interested parties.
- Refine a roadmap of improvement moving forward and gain buy-in.

A word of caution: We have noticed over time that many organizations are suffering from "assessment fatigue." In short, too many assessments on too many areas of the organization and people become "tired" of questionnaires. Additionally, there is a level of uncertainty as to what "management" will do with the information collected. To be blunt, many people believe negative information will be used to "beat them about the head and shoulders." Managers too, often shy away from assessments because such surveys often point out, sometimes glaringly, inefficiencies, negligence of core practices, lack of key tools and techniques, assignment of inexperienced personnel to critical projects, among other issues. Assessments, to many, have the specter of an audit, and no one wants to be audited. Many people really believe that the definition of an auditor is "someone who shows up after the battle and shoots the wounded"!

To encourage participation, the assessment must be promoted and used as a tool or instrument for developmental purposes; it is not in anyone's best interest to use an assessment for evaluation purposes for such important considerations as compensation, promotion, demotion, and the like. This is why it is critical that a key executive sponsor, one who is well known and respected throughout the organization, be visible in all aspects of the assessment.

Ultimately, how "management" uses the results will speak volumes about the true nature of the exercise. Used properly, assessment data can yield major improvements and help an organization boost its success in program management.

Final Thoughts

The purpose of the Levin-Ward Program Management Complexity Model is to help develop the competencies of organizations and program managers to promote greater effectiveness in overcoming program complexity and ensuring delivery of proposed program benefits. Often, the complex aspects of the program are not discovered until the program is well into the executing phase or the delivery of program benefits phase in the life cycle, especially if new technology is in use. Unfortunately, by then it can be too late to manage such complexity. In short, the program manager, or organization, becomes overwhelmed with issue after issue, progress grinds to a halt, and the costs begin to skyrocket.

Based on the authors' experience, organizations of all types and sizes have recognized that many of their initiatives fall under the definition of a program, yet they are managing these important pieces of work as separate, stand-alone projects. As such, they are missing the "big picture," and are probably not gaining efficiencies, economies of scale, or optimizing resources as could be the case if they were managing the effort as a coherent "whole." Most importantly, key interdependencies can be missed, and seemingly small perturbations in one project can have a major impact on several others. When managed as a whole one stands a greater chance of understanding how projects relate in many ways and at many levels. In short, there is a better, more effective way to manage them.

The number of different stakeholders involved in programs, especially working with Program Governance Boards or Steering Committees, only adds to the challenges faced by the program manager. A program manager can become consumed with stakeholder communications at all levels to a point where he or she spends more time communicating progress and issues related to the program than actually managing the program itself. Proactive stakeholder management is essential for overall program success.

As programs increase in size and complexity, it is easy to become bombarded with information that is not required and to miss the critical metrics and indicators of project or program success. Also, it is easy in such a fast-paced environment to overlook the requirements of some critical stakeholders in the program life cycle. Other challenges increase with the global environment of many programs and also with the increased use of outsourcing, which often leads to a larger number of suppliers. On many programs, face-to-face meetings will not occur.

While program management is becoming the progression of choice and the next level in the project management career path in many organizations, the roles and responsibilities of the program manager have often not been defined. In fact, the authors have worked with organizations that cannot define program management, cannot distinguish the roles and responsibilities of a program manager from a project manager, and where the title program managers seems to be freely distributed to just about anyone managing any piece of work. Such lack of structure serves as an obstacle to promoting sound program management practices and developing personal competencies in those individuals who legitimately manage programs as opposed to projects. In short, *program management* is often a term without meaning.

The knowledge, skills, and competencies of the program manager, however, differ greatly from that of the project manager. For example, team members may be unclear as to why their specific project is part of the program in the first place and why it is being managed in a program structure. They may not recognize the benefits that can be derived from a program management approach and may not know how their specific project relates to other projects in the program.

They may wonder whether or not they will interact with the program manager and, if so, how often this interaction will occur. It is necessary for the program manager to ensure that team members do not lose sight of the overall vision or end state and maintain momentum to complete the required activities. The program manager also must work actively with those involved in portfolio management to ensure that his or her program continues to support the organization's strategic goals and objectives.

Additionally, because of global competition and technological obsolescence, as well as the natural tendency for stakeholders to change their ideas on priorities, program managers must continually make changes and show they are willing to embrace change. While change is to be expected in today's environment, its timing, however, is uncertain. The program manager must be a change agent for the organization.

Program management remains in its infancy as a profession as compared to project management. While a wealth of information has been written over the years on project management, the same cannot be said of program management. However, the program management profession is gaining attention through the development of the Program Management Standard (PMI, 2008d), certification of individuals as PgMPs®, and the recognition by organizations that use of programs can provide more benefits than if their component projects are managed in stand-alone fashion.

The complexity inherent in large programs requires further study so that useful tools, techniques, and approaches can be successfully applied by organizations and their program managers. After all, large and complex programs are undertaken by organizations to meet the challenging strategic objectives established by key executives in order to keep the organization prosperous, relevant, and a source of continued investment by shareholders and customers alike. The Levin-Ward model is a first step in identifying competencies critical for success in dealing with program complexity. Its use by organizations, program managers, and prospective program managers will uncover areas where greater focus is needed to boost chances of program success. It's not a "silver bullet," but we hope it leads you in a direction of greater success. Please let us know how it works out!

References

Alderman, N., Ivory, C., and Vaughan, R. (2005). Sense-making as a process within complex service-led projects. *International Journal of Project Management, 23,* 380–385.

Association for Project Management (2006). *APM body of knowledge,* 5th ed. High Wycombe, Buckinghamshire, U.K: Association for Project Management.

Austin, S., Newton, A., Steele, J., and Waskett, P. (2002). Modeling and managing project complexity. *International Journal of Project Management 20,* 191–198.

Baccarini, D. (1996). The concept of project complexity—A review. *International Journal of Project Management, 14*(4), 201–204.

Balestrero, G. (2010). Project management continues to add value in times of economic stress. Presentation to the R.E.P. Breakfast, Melbourne, Australia. 22 February 2010.

Bannan, K. J. (2006). It's a snap. *PM Network, 20(5),* 78–83.

Bartlett, J. (2000). *Managing programmes of business change.* Hampshire, Great Britain: Project Manager Today Publications.

Central Computer and Telecommunications Agency. (1999). *Managing successful programmes.* London, England: The Stationery Office.

Cicmil, S., Cooke-Davies, T., Crawford, L., and Richardson, K. (2009). *Exploring the complexity of projects: Implications of complexity theory for project management practice.* Newtown Square, PA: Project Management Institute.

Cleland, D.I., and Gareis, R. (2006). *Global project management handbook.* New York, NY: The McGraw-Hill Companies.

Cooke-Davies, T., Cicmil, S., Crawford, L., and Richardson, K. (2007). We're not in Kansas anymore Toto: Mapping the strange landscape of complexity theory, and its relationship to project management. *Project Management Journal, 38(2),* 50–61.

Crawford, L. (2005). Senior management perceptions of project management competence. *International Journal of Project Management, 27(1),* 7–16.

Defense Systems Management College. (1990). *A competency model of program managers in the DoD acquisition process.* Washington, DC: Defense Systems Management College.

Dombkins, D.H., Editor. (2006). *Competency standard for complex project managers.* Sydney Australia: Australian Institute of Project Management.

Flannes, S., and Levin, G. (2005). *Essential people skills for project managers.* Vienna, VA: Management Concepts.

Gareis, R., and Nankivel, J. (2007). Competency vs. Connection, *PM Network, 21(7),* 56–58.

Geraldi, J. (2008). Patterns of complexity: the thermometer of complexity. *Project Perspectives, Vol. XXIX,* 4–9.

Helm, J., and Remington, K. (2005). Effective project sponsorship, an evaluation of the role of the executive sponsor in complex infrastructure projects by senior project managers. *Project Management Journal, 36(3),* 51–61.

Ivory, C., and Alderman, N. (2005). Can project management learn anything from studies of failure in complex systems? *Project Management Journal, 36(3),* 5–16.

Jaafari, A. (2003). Project management in the age of complexity and change. *Project Management Journal, 34(4),* 47–57.

Levin, G., and Green, A. (2009). *Implementing program management.* Boca Raton, FL: CRC Press.

Levin, G. (2010). *Interpersonal skills for portfolio, program, and project managers.* Vienna, VA: Management Concepts.

Maylor, H., Vidgen, R., and Carver, S. (2008). Managerial complexity in project-based operations: a grounded model and its implications for practice. *Project Management Journal, 39(S1),* S2–S134.

Miller, R., and Hobbs, B. (2005). Governance regimes for large complex projects. *Project Management Journal, 36(3),* 42–50.

Milosevic, D.Z., Martinelli, R.J., and Waddell, J.M. (2007). *Program management for improved business results.* Hoboken, NJ: John Wiley & Sons, Inc.

Office of Government Commerce. (2007). *Managing successful programmes,* London, England: The Stationery Office.

Partinton, D., Pellegrinelli, S., and Young, M. (2005). Attributes of programme management competence: An interpretive study. *International Journal of Project Management, 23(2),* 87–96.

Pascale, R.T. (1999). Surfing the edge of chaos. *Sloan Management Review.* http://sloanreview.mit.edu/the-magazine/articles/1999/spring/4038/surfing-the-edge-of-chaos/ {accessed December 28, 2008}.

Pascale, R., Milleman, M., and Gioja, L. (2000). *Surfing the edge of chaos: The laws of nature and the new laws of business.* New York, NY: Three Rivers Press.

Patanakul, P., and Milosevic, D. (2009). The effectiveness in managing a group of multiple projects: factors of influence and measurement criteria. *International Journal of Project Management, 27(3)*, 216–233.

Pellegrinelli, S., Partington, D., Hemingway, C., Mohdzain, Z., and Shah, M. (2007). The importance of context in programme management: An empirical review of programme practices. *International Journal of Project Management, 25(1)*, 41–55.

Pich, M.T., Loch, C.H., and De Meyer, A. (2002). On uncertainty, ambiguity, and complexity in project management. *Management Science, 48(8)*, 1008–1023.

Project Management Institute. (2006). *Program management professional examination specification.* Newtown Square, PA: Project Management Institute.

Project Management Institute. (2007). *Project manager competency development framework, second edition.* Newtown Square, PA: Project Management Institute.

Project Management Institute. (2008a). *A guide to the project management body of knowledge (PMBOK® Guide), fourth edition.* Newtown Square, PA: Project Management Institute.

Project Management Institute. (2008b). *Organizational project management maturity model (OPM3), second edition.* Newtown Square, PA: Project Management Institute.

Project Management Institute. (2008c). *The standard for portfolio management, second edition.* Newtown Square, PA: Project Management Institute.

Project Management Institute. (2008d). *The standard for program management, second edition.* Newtown Square, PA: Project Management Institute.

Project Management Institute. (2010). *GAC update.* E-mail. Leslie.Higham @ pmi.org, received 30 September, 2010.

Remington, K., and Pollack, J. (2007). *Tools for complex projects.* Aldershot, Hampshire, U.K.: Gower Publishing Ltd.

Rittinghouse, J.W. (2001). *Program management for corporate information technology leaders.* Haverford, PA: Infinity Publishing.

Sanghera, P. (2008). *Fundamentals of effective program management: A process approach based on the global standard.* Fort Lauderdale, FL: J. Ross Publishing.

Standish Group International. (2007). *CHAOS report 2007: The laws of chaos.* Boston, MA: The Standish Group International.

Thomas, J., and Mengel, T. (2008). Preparing project managers to deal with complexity—advanced project management education. *International Journal of Project Management, (26)3*, 304–315.

United States Government Accountability Office. (2003). Best Practices. *Better support of weapon system program managers needed for impressive outcomes.* Washington, D.C.: United States Government Accountability Office.

United States Government Accountability Office. (2007). *Cost assessment guide: Best practices for estimating and managing program costs.* Washington, D.C.: United States Government Accountability Office.

Ward, J.L. (2009). Programs are not projects: Boosting program management effectiveness. *2009 PMI Global Congress Proceedings*, Orlando, FL.

Whitty, S.J., and Maylor, H. (2009). And then came complex project management (revised). *International Journal of Project Management, 27(3),* 304–310.

Williams, D., and Parr, T. (2006). *Enterprise programme management.* Basingstoke, Hampshire, U.K.: Palgrave MacMillan.

Williams, T.M. (1999). The need for new paradigms for complex projects. *International Journal of Project Management, 17(5),* 269–273.

Index